Black X

Black X

Liberatory Thought in Azania

Tendayi Sithole

WITS UNIVERSITY PRESS

Published in South Africa by:
Wits University Press
1 Jan Smuts Avenue
Johannesburg 2001

www.witspress.co.za

First published 2024

http://dx.doi.org.10.18772/12024028684

978-1-77614-868-4 (Paperback)
978-1-77614-869-1 (Hardback)
978-1-77614-870-7 (Web PDF)
978-1-77614-871-4 (EPUB)

This publication is peer reviewed following international best practice standards
for academic and scholarly books.

The financial assistance of the National Institute for the Humanities and Social
Sciences (NIHSS) towards this publication is hereby acknowledged. Opinions
expressed and those arrived at are those of the author and should not necessarily
be attributed to the NIHSS.

NATIONAL INSTITUTE
FOR THE HUMANITIES
AND SOCIAL SCIENCES

Project manager: Karen Press
Copyeditor: Karen Press
Proofreader: Inga Norenius
Indexer: Sanet le Roux
Cover design: Hybrid Creative
Typeset in 10.5 point Crimson

For Nyikayese

Contents

Tomorrow is cancelled.
—The Invisible Committee, *Now*

This place won't be here in the morning.
—Frank B. Wilderson III, *Incognegro: Memoir of Exile and Apartheid*

Azania should be thought again and against the grain of enclosure and its attendant sterility, so that there is liberation.

Even at this moment that is coined as the aftermath of apartheid, which is to say, the post-1994 South Africa, the name of the country is one of the scandalous issues that still persists. Not that this is a boiling contention, but it is a fundamental issue that refuses any form of forgetting. Since this aftermath is that of forgetting, the work of remembering is done by those who not only still yearn for the renaming of South Africa, but insist on exposing its racist machinations, and do not believe in the myth that it is a non-racial polity which has surpassed settler-colonialism. This work of remembering is a continuous task that is carried out by those who not only refute the idea of South Africa as a non-racial polity, but are still calling for South Africa as a non-racial polity to come to an end so as to give birth to Azania. This is the country's rightful name, chosen by those who were conquered and who, by structure and design, were racialized as not forming part of the polity. It is key, therefore, to note that this is a problematic of those who have been structurally unaddressed. In the present South Africa, there is no ethical duty to deal with the memory of the long arc of black

1

dispossession, and to confront the re-engineering of racism in its perverse and dissimulated forms.

Given the preoccupation with 'apartheid', there is a systematic form of dissimulation and also that induced forgetting that there were regimes that preceded it, and that, by its nature, apartheid served as the heightened perfection of these antecedent regimes. What came to be the territory called South Africa is a country whose name has been legally designed through conquest. This, then, should be understood as the structured logic that has meant black dispossession. Is apartheid not preceded by settler-colonialism, slavery and segregation? Why is there no insistence on making this common sense, just like the evocation of apartheid? Is South Africa the name of the polity that has defined itself by means of the denial of the black? Is South Africa not a territory that should be understood through its long historical arc? Why is there a fixation on the significance of apartheid, as if the conquest of the black started in 1948 and ended in 1994? Is it not ethical to backdate the audit to the start of this historical arc?

The name South Africa, thus considered with a different disposition and temperament, invites a way of thinking from a black point of view. In doing so, the effort is to make it clear that the black point of view is a radical one, one not underwritten by liberal conformism, which valorizes non-racialism and thus, sordidly, accuses any demand for freedom voiced from this point of view of being 'regressive' or, ridiculously so, 'racist'. This, obviously, borders on nothing but blackmail stemming from liberal guilt and other conservative attachments that continue to be apologetic for conquest, and forever remain silent on the subject of white privilege and black dispossession.

By way of formulation and elaboration, it is worth setting out to think through the word and world of Azania. Azania is not just the name that must necessarily replace South Africa. It goes further to propose a set of conceptual principalities that should be sufficient to address the multifaceted, interconnected, interpenetrated, integrated word and world of Azania, in all its complex folds and unfoldings of form and the content of its discursive marks. What is undertaken here is the teasing out of a few themes, which are part of the larger whole.

Azania is the name that has been insisted upon by the black and its call is still forever urgent. It is in this insistence and call that the present intervention is located. It follows in the lines of the radical expression of ideas of the Pan Africanist Congress, led by Robert Sobukwe, and the Black Consciousness Movement, led by Steve Biko. Instead of calling this country South Africa, both the Pan Africanist Congress and the Black Consciousness Movement opted for a different name, refusing to conform to apartheid and its parallel liberal conformism. Up to this current conjuncture, the call for Azania still stands, and it can be said to be a spectral affair. It serves as the point of interruption of liberal conformism, which even claims that South Africa is a clean slate – 'new South Africa', 'post-apartheid', 'our democracy', and, more absurdly, 'the Rainbow Nation'. South Africa is still a settler-colony, an antiblack polity, and that is why liberal conformism is there to dissimulate antiblackness and the blatant continuities of its settler-colonialist logics.

In making a case for Azania, this meditation stems from a different point of view. The lived experience of being black is a view of something, of somewhere – a point of view denied – the black point of view qua X. It is one standpoint, an existential grounding. Lewis Gordon (1995, 31) warns that 'a view from nowhere isn't a view at all'. So, the black point of view is a lived point of view, a *locus standi*. This is what Azania is. Its Pan Africanist Congress and Black Consciousness Movement affinities and traces have a continuity in the present which takes nothing as analogous, but as radically different from South Africa. However, the focus of this meditation will take as its point of departure the Pan Africanist Congress, which then handed the baton to the Black Consciousness Movement, and extend right up to the present where these two formations have seen, after the post-1994 ballot box exercise, liberal conformism and factionalism along party-political lines. What is of interest is that the word and world of Azania, to prove that it is the strand of black thought, still haunts the corridors of the post-1994 idea of South Africa. That is why George Wauchope (1984) affirms that Azania is the land of the free black people, and there cannot be Azania if there is no freedom. Since there is a yearning for freedom even now, its call is in the name of Azania. In short, to evoke freedom is to evoke Azania, and vice versa. In this continued settler-colonialism that has disguised itself with a black government and the Constitution, the call for Azania still endures. To amplify Wauchope's words, Azania is yet to come.

What unfolds here is a meditation that is incisive and deci-sive, charged and antagonistic. It is where 'X' emerges as the mark of the black point of view.

Still, why X? Indeed, the emergence of X comes from different markers and significations, but it is also a contrarian position if it is affirmed from the black point of view. It is the idea of thinking black, a disposition that makes it clear that South Africa, as it is, not only stands for the name that carries with it its settler-colonial baggage, but is a polity that is funda-mentally antiblack, even in its self-declared 'non-racial' liberal democratic constitutionalism. That is why its passions of liberal conformism always run high when the black point of view is affirmed and expressed, because it does not want to see the role of its crowding-out tendency and whitewashing position, and

4

its defence of the idea of South Africa as a clean slate, exposed. That is why it is an investment that dissimulates the reality of antiblackness while flaunting liberty, equality and justice. From the disposition of X, there is a need to engage in another mode of critical discourse that is outside the post-1994 common sense and its passionate defence of the status quo (the famous clichés being 'defending the Constitution', 'cherishing our hard-won freedoms', and the irony being that what is defended and cherished does not address the problem of antiblackness that continues to plague this polity).

Undoubtedly, Azania is not taken for granted by those who affirm it. This, again, is X, and it is in the name of the country that is not there, because it is the country that is yet to come after the obliteration of South Africa. This X is the mark of what has been denied, and it is the mark of the polity that has suffered continued dehumanization, even up to the present under the rule of the African National Congress, which claims to be a black ruling political party. Sure, the African National Congress claims to have brought liberation, and it has birthed a new South Africa, the 'Rainbow Nation', and a so-called non-racial polity. The concern is not with how the African National Congress has failed, but with a different point of view that affirms Azania, and why it is a polity that will be birthed through the liberation that confronts the continuing settler-colonialism and the antiblackness that continues to underwrite this idea of South Africa. The name Azania, as the problematic of X, means evoking the name that is seen as a scandalous challenge to the order of things, and a truth that should always be ridiculed, if not muzzled, by those who propagate the idea of South Africa. Or, strangely, if its evocation is seen as a mere rhetorical prop, a form of cheap political point-scoring by those who have no investment in it, this is done deliberately to render the name impotent and unnecessary. It is not, however, strange that the name Azania has suffered bastard-ization at the hands of the African National Congress and its refusal to have the name of the country changed. The truth of the matter is that the African National Congress did not come up with the name, and it will not allow a name coined by the Pan Africanist Congress and Black Consciousness Movement to prevail.

The renaming of the country is a matter that lies outside the agenda of the African National Congress. It is against this reality that the call for liberation gets heightened, because what the African National Congress sees as change is what the Pan Africanist Congress and Black Consciousness see as stasis. It is not only the change of the name of the country that is demanded by the black, since, of course, South Africa can be renamed Azania and yet still remain settler-colonialist in its structure and design. The call for Azania, obviously, comes from the radical tradition that confronts the settler-colonialist logics that inform the idea of South Africa. There is no need, therefore, to try to fix the scandal of liberal conformism, as this is the order that does not have, in its originary and original sense, the idea of a black polity in mind.

It is in this discursive frame that Azania is called by its rightful name by those who, in their rightful name, have the atti-tudinal stance and are asserting the outlook of blackness. For in fact, Azania to them, having been birthed at the conjuncture and on the trajectory of the struggle for what Mogobe Ramose (1991) reformulates clearly as 'self-determination' (which is the right of the conquered to call themselves by their own name, and from the radical stance of wanting to name the land of their birth), also means dislodging the country and its name from the tenta-cles of conquest. Self-determination, following Ramose, is what Azania is, and those who wage the existential struggle of/for its word and world are embarking on a fundamental and necessary task that is in need of commitment and responsibility. Blacks know that freedom cannot be given on a silver platter. They must fight for it. Their historical and contemporary dispossession is at the centre of things, and what they have been dispossessed of must be repaired and restored to them. Azania is predicated on the question of freedom in its authentic and absolute form, as opposed to the freedom declared in post-1994 South Africa, where blacks are still landless.

The idea of South Africa, according to Ramose (2018), is founded on conquest. Taking this point further, Haunani Trask (2004, 10) writes that 'colonialism began with conquest and is today maintained by a settler administration created out of the doctrine of cultural hierarchy'. Ramose (2018) correctly states that the doctrine of Discovery – the international law of settler colonialism, the justification for its expansionist logic in conquering other lands and subjugating the indigenous people of those lands – was deployed to make war for conquest, as if the indigenous people did not exist, and were simply disposed of as nothing but surplus labour that fed the desires of the conquerors. This doctrine, Ramose affirms, is the complementary edifice of the just war doctrine turned unjust war doctrine. The just war doctrine refers to situations in which two states or antagonists engage in a declared war that is seen as just, even if it is often asymmetrical, and results in victory and defeat. The unjust war, on the other hand, is one in which defeat is a priori; it is nothing but the settler-colonial invasion, with its firepower, of the indigenous people. It is a war that is undeclared by the indigenous people, and can even lead to genocidal elimination and annihilation. There is nothing foreign about the doctrine of Discovery in this continuing present. Conquest is unleashed under the ethical suspension of the unjust war doctrine, which then legitimizes 'the right of conquest [based] on the doctrine of Discovery' (Ramose 2018, 340).

The law, as mobilized by settler-colonialism, is the extensive elaboration and justification of 'customary law', which was a colonial invention and fabrication, and such a 'force of law', according to Mahmood Mamdani (2013, 46), cemented the 'technology of colonial governance'. Tradition was enforced to intensify colonial power, but the command was to use 'civil law' as the governing code. This is the indirect rule that Mamdani refers to as 'define' and 'rule'. Conquest is direct, and those who are placed at the front to oversee customary law serve as a mask for the colonial law that commands them. As Mamdani (1996) notes, customary law was subjected to the limits of the colonial state, which he terms the 'central state', and this was applied through a 'repugnancy clause' that was applied differently in various colonies. But the fundamental form of rule was colonial rule.

> Direct and indirect rule was not two consecutive phases in the development of colonial governance. Though the accent shifted from direct to indirect rule, the two continued in tandem: the civilizing mission (assimilation) existed alongside the management of difference (pluralism). The language of the civilizing mission shifted from the evangelical to the secular; its practice shifted from religious conversion to spreading the rule of law. (Mamdani 2013, 45)

But all this is nothing but conquest. The shifts, more qualitatively, can be seen as semantic ones. What Mamdani brings to the fore is that this technology brought with it 'civil law', and it was used to entrench difference as this has been the central motif of conquest. 'Law is central to the project that seeks to manage and reproduce difference' (Mamdani 2013, 44). Customary law is just a fetish; it is the law that only applies as a force to those who are conquered, in order to make them further subject themselves. The speech of customary law is nothing but a deputized speech that is mute in the face of what is called civil law.

Conquest, as Ramose (2018) states, has been the authorial and authorized signature. There is thought, and it is not thinking the production of life, but the thought of conquest. It lies there in the logics of conquest. This thought is not thinking, as its source, articulation, expression, direction and destination are the black body in relation to which sadism rouses its passions. In apt terms, Anthony Farley states:

> The production of knowledge concerning the black body is a process by which whites exorcise their own demons, and is, therefore a pleasure in itself. If the black body is the site and cite of all ills, then the white body is not. The black body is the result of this convergence of power, knowledge, and pleasure. The discourse of race, then, is itself a discourse of pleasure-humiliation. (Farley 1997, 475)

This discourse is a war on the black. It is a war that Ramose (2018) captures as an unjust war, a war of conquest. As a result of this unjust war, made legible by law, the very idea of South Africa, the economy of its signs, proliferates and one such deadly result is stripping the conquered of all that has to do with their existence. Dispossession is installed, and it is in this dispossession that the discourse of pleasure–humiliation has sadistically enacted, acted and actualized itself. In this diabolical form, the dispossession of land, labour and humanity is legalized. The economy of signs invents X as the construction of blackness by whiteness. X is the being of no name. It is the being-of-no-being – of nothing(ness). It is the black being othered as nothing in so far as personhood is concerned, that fundamental erasure as a being in South Africa which places the black outside it, as 'inert props', to follow Frank Wilderson (2020, 15), where representation has proven to be repression. What, then, does blackness mean in this construction of conquest? Obviously, in attending to blackness, X will mean the address of the non-addressable form. If there is address, there is nothing that this address is directed towards. In this instance, then, to address the black is to address the X, nothing qua nothingness, or in terms of what Aimé Césaire (1972, 42) conceptualizes as 'thingification' (where those who conquered have turned their victims into things, and nothing has happened as there was no one there – say, *nothing at all*). In this thingification, in the discourse of conquest, the black is what Farley (1997, 457) calls a 'fetish object', which has meant being structured in terms of asymmetrical non-relational ontological forces where white pleasure is derived and extracted from black pain.

X, from the violent thingification of conquest and its accompanying racist mechanics and machinations, has come to be, in Frantz Fanon's terms (1967, 151), the designation and presentation of a 'phobogenic object'. According to David Marriott (2007, 207), the black is 'shaped by an introjected and anxiety-producing fear of being attacked – both within and without – by phobic intrusions'. These come from white racist fantasies, which are then projected onto the black body as a field of battle. It is where what Marriott terms the 'racial *imago*' (2007, 208) emerges, and the X is imposed on the black as a sign of intrusion, displacement and fixation. It is a result of this construction that, in its intent and purposes, has to serve a double function. First, blacks are hated by racists. And second, as a result of that hate, blacks are supposed to hate themselves and, more absurdly, love the racists who hate them. Here is an indictment presented by Jared Sexton:

> You live a valueless form of life whose value exists as potential in and of another world, a higher-dimensional space. You cannot protect yourself and you will not be saved. You will learn that lesson to the young ones and pass it on to them as a mission or a curse. You cannot protect them with your love or advice and no one has yet devised an art of war sufficient to the task. (Sexton 2015, 162)

The colonial construction of the black as nothing sentient, an object among many other objects, to evoke Fanon (1967), is the reality that has been cemented through and through. This is a way of writing the bodily being of the black as the realm of the *exteriori*. The black is relegated to the category of those, as Sexton (2006, 251) states, assigned as the 'problem people, dwelling at the absence of human presence'. As Marriott (2007, 209) notes, 'the sense of being hated from within also seems inseparable from the condition of being hated from without'. There is nothing out there but a void. The black is hated to such an extent that it is an image and not a living embodiment of being. Marriott (2000, 12) puts it thus: 'An image of hate, a hated image'. Blackness is just a fixed sign – a sign of nothing. This is the nothing of politics and nothing of being. The black has to emerge, in its existential figuration, from the point of view that denies it as a point of view. This is done to deliberately make blackness hate itself. Out of the condition of necessitating its mode of being, blackness refigures its own terms, and thus makes X something different from what has been whitely imposed.

Blackness, as X, assumes not only a different meaning, designation, sign to whatever is in the racist fantasy and imagination. By dislodging itself from everything that stands in the name of representation, as Marriott (2018a) shows, the designation of the X of blackness assumes a radical dimension in at least two interrelated ways. One, X is what Fanon (1967, 109) calls the 'fact of blackness', where the concern is not with seeking recognition and not with bowing to the dictates of the 'white gaze' (1967, 109). And two, X is what Biko (1978) called for in Black Consciousness, which came as the result of breaking from the patronage and tutelage of white liberals who claimed to be 'friends of the blacks' and 'feeling black pain', but insisted that they would represent blacks. In encountering themselves as conscious, the vanguard of Black Consciousness must sever themselves from white liberals, as they were now becoming *being-in-themselves* and *being-for-themselves*. The inauguration of other encounters is what becomes manifest. Here is Jacques Derrida:

> Encounter *is* separation. Such a proposition, which contradicts 'logic', breaks the unity of Being – which resides in the fragile link of the 'is' – by welcoming the other and difference into the source of meaning. But, it will be said, Being must always already be conceptualized in order to say these things – the encounter and the separation of what and of whom – and especially in order to say that encounter *is* separation. (Derrida 1978, 74, emphasis in the original)

Marriott's formulation of X is a different construction altogether. For Marriott, this X is not of representation, but the critique and obligation of representation. It is in representation that the black is, according to Fanon (1967, 220), 'acted upon', having no capacity to name itself and also the cause of its suffering, including its *politico-ontologico* demands. The problem of representation is the way one is seen, constructed and then presented.

In the different reconfiguration that blackness enacts, it coming to X and being that X, the whole referential act changes. It is not a matter of the black being referred to by whiteness (representation), but of the self-referentiality of the black (intrapersonally and interpersonally). That is why Marriott (2018b, 398) is on point in saying that 'to the extent that the X can never be named or spoken of (and so is not a metaphor or a prosopopoeia), its strangeness cannot, as such, be represented but remains uncertain as to its knowledge and manufacture'. Here, blackness is not in the clutches of racist speech in so far as X is concerned.

> Blackness would then be inseparable from the effect of a certain nonknowing whose expression changes the very nature of what we think we know, or experience, as black. Indeed, this would suggest that the signifier blackness must remain necessarily innocent of the very notion of its innocence, for to know it is to discover a blackness that is undecidable, irretrievable. (Marriott 2018b, 357)

For, in fact, it is no longer the reference of the racist speech (representation), but of its own codes.

> Between simile and metaphor, the distance at first appears so wide as to be unbridgeable. Yet the two figures manage to exist side by side without being reducible to the other. But what is it that allows one to pass from the other? Is it not the figure of politics

that allows this focus on each separately? Or is politics precisely the literalization of the gap to coincide in a new historical meaning? Considered a trope, it overcomes racist separation. (Marriott 2018b, 400)

The blackness of X, the mark that is deployed here from now on as X, the idea of the proper, is the reconfiguration that will unfold as a form of blackness in its own name, by its own name, for its own name, with its own name, and with all that is naming which comes from blackness as the site of affirmation, the attitude of Azania itself, its modalities of inscription notwithstanding.

What is it that lies in the form and content of this reconfiguration of Azania? This is an opening. The 'figure of the X', as Nahum Chandler (2014, 62) states, 'has been placed at its opening'. Here, X is not a conditional quotidian position, but a living embodiment, a new arrangement, the whole reconfiguration that Fred Moten (2018b) has declared to be the blackness of being as the operative function that instantiates X – what precedes and accompanies it. This opening has a rupturous force that Chandler (2014, 69) refers to as 'a certain kind of response, indeed, a violent, destructive, response'. To counter antiblackness, the figure of the X institutes modalities of critique through the rewriting of the episteme. Colonial conquest is problematized by the figure of the X as a form of beginning, 'another beginning', as Chandler (2014, 126) states, and also, 'beginning otherwise'. The installation of X, as Chandler authorizes, is not nothing or absence; it is the order in which the rewriting of the episteme will mean the asking of unasked questions by the figure whose humanity has been subjected to perpetual questioning. And this is a radical attitude that stands in opposition to representation, which is only concerned with the meaning of that X, as if blacks who took and affirm it seek to be legible to this 'unconscious consensus' (the very idea of representation proper which has no concern for black pain but is only narcissistically invested in denialism [Wilderson 2020, 12]) with its racist machinations.

The X is seized from what Fanon (1967, 109) calls the 'white gaze', as blackness has not internalized the racist projections and introjections, and thus does not become the spectral entity of the thing seen (the black of black) and not seen (the non-human). The white gaze is the gaze of the masked face. The face that does not want to be seen. It is the face of what Derrida (1978, 74) captures 'as difference and within dissimulation'. The X is, then, rooted in the stance that it will not allow itself to act and submit to the ways it is seen by the white gaze; it will not care what that gaze thinks and there will be no effort to seek recognition from that gaze. X, far from being severed from representation, is not an end but a means.

In having to account for black thought in Azania, and the critical unfolding of what X is, this book is structured in a way that gives a different account of its thematic concerns to that of the liberal conformism that saturates the South African critical discourse.

Chapter 1, 'The Black and the Colonial Contract', undertakes a systematic critique of the concept of a contract, thus situating it in its colonial fold – that is, the force that encloses critical thought and saturates it with investment in the liberal conformism. In so doing, the case is made that the colonial contract is not, at all, a contract. For, it is devoid of any form of relation with the black. The chapter exposes the non-relational nature of the black and the colonial contract, and it is here that black critique is mobilized to expose this ontological scandal. The chapter, in its systematic examination of why the colonial contract is not a contract, considers what the black point of view is in having to criticize this formation. This criticism goes to the extent of criticizing the death contract as something that the black cannot enter into.

Chapter 2, 'On Land and Being', engages with the land question in South Africa, and its argument is that there is a need to account for the subjectivities of this question. Land is looked at from the perspective of being, as opposed to mechanistic forms such as market forces, policy and constitutional issues which reinforce liberal conformism. The chapter engages with the discursive register whose point of departure is the ontological question of being. This further allows for the lived experience of blackness to confront the long historical arc of conquest, and what is made clear is that the land question has (re)produced white privilege and black dispossession.

Chapter 3, 'Steve Biko: The Matter of Ante-Marx(ism)', is an elaborate critique of Marx and Marxism, carried out from the perspective of Steve Biko's philosophical thought. At the core of this chapter is the argument that Marx and Marxism are confronted by the question of colonial conquest and since this is disavowed, they remain inadequate in their understanding of antiblackness. The chapter locates Biko in the Azanian existential tradition in order to make the case that his philosophy is relevant, and it presents a discursive critique of Marx and Marxists, who aim to whitewash black ontological misery through their valorization of class and disavowal of antiblack racism.

Chapter 4, 'Mabogo P. More's Intensifications', explores the question of the stakes of blackness in relation to dehumanization. The chapter deploys the concept of intensification to argue that as a form of radical insistence, intensification confronts ontological fabrication, and is the force that animates the existential struggle. Intensification, this chapter argues, is the totality of More's philosophical anthropology, and this makes him a non-conformist philosopher as he radically critiques antiblackness. It is through intensification that More asserts his humanity and refuses to be complicit in any form of dehumanization.

The book closes with a 'Postscript: The "X File" (Notes on Extended Thought)', to suggest that there is no closure, as insisted on by liberal conformism, but the radical opening that comes through revisiting the concept of X not merely as a matter of thought. This chapter acts as a form of disclosure of the criticality of black thought, and articulates a critique that cements the black point of view as necessary for the word and world of Azania. It is in this elaborated extension that X is conceptualized and refigured as the X of blackness, and it is here that it is given its lived force against conquest.

1 | The Black and the Colonial Contract

There is no relation between the black and the colonial contract because the black is expelled from anything that stands for relationality.

What exists is the weight of imposition and a contradiction in all things that might be termed 'contractual', because of the absence of relation. This non-relation has been part of what South Africa is. This is the territory that has been founded on conquest, which is underwritten by the colonial contract. Therefore, the colonial contract is not, at all, a contract. In real terms, there is no relation present in what is colonial and what is a colonial contract. This is the exposition that is brought by the idea of Azania. If there is anything that is called relation, that is nothing but a myth. Colonialism, the colonial contract, is imposed as if there are parties to it, whereas there are none – there is no contract between parties. The colonial contract does not offer anything. It takes away everything. It has no system of relation, and there is nothing symmetrical about it; the black is disadvantaged not because of being a non-party to the colonial contract but because of being the *exterior* – the non-contractual thing. There is surplus imposition, excess even, as the colonial violence is the legitimizing point of extraction, looting, dispossession and death. By being ratified by law, the colonial apparatus par excellence, the colonial contract is a foreclosure of the black narrative that criticizes what it has witnessed and experienced, because the black does not have the ontological status of subjecthood.

The colonial contract is a totality that unleashes terror in its unimaginable excess. It is the imposition of power that legitimizes dispossession, dehumanization and death. Also, it is underwritten by the infrastructure of antiblackness. What is a problem, therefore, is colonial conquest as the authorizing mode of this contract. It is in the name of colonial conquest that there is a colonial contract.

The colonial contract is not a point of reference. It is, in point of fact, an object of critique from the perspective of the figure of the black. For it is the contract that confronts the black as the de-ontologized entity, the one dethroned from the ranks of humanity and consigned to the abyss – the domain of non-existence. It is clear from the Azanian disposition that the black did not agree to be the object of colonization. Brutal force has been used to subjugate the black into colonial submission. At no moment did the black sign a contract to be subjected to the perpetual state of unfreedom and dehumanization. The idea of South Africa has the colonial signature as an inscription that is fraudulent – a forgery *tout court* – for it is underwritten by the logic of colonial conquest which, in reality, does not need any consenting parties to settle any form of agreement. It is just a surprise; it is done at will, and it is based on asymmetrical power arrangements that facilitate colonial conquest. The system of markings that comes in the form of a signature authorizing the contract to legitimize its deceit and trickery, which then pass as truth authorized by law, consists of inscriptions that deny the black any form of ontological status. A contract is known to involve parties who assume the ontological status of signatories, but this does not apply to the colonial contract, as the black is not a signatory or party to it. Of course, the contract does not always have to be egalitarian, since it is underwritten by asymmetrical power arrangements. For the black, these arrangements are fraudulently binding, and they are implemented as such.

The materiality of the contract is rendered immaterial to the black. The black might be contractually bound, but this means that the black has no terms to set, not having entered into an agreement because of the imposed non-relational status with things pronounced through contractual clauses. To enter into a contract as a signatory or party means being bound by it and thus knowing its terms and conditions (perhaps its fine print and even obscure, legal jargon-based clauses). These clauses are so closed that there is no way of entering them. They are clauses that close relations. They are clauses of non-relations – the very things that bring the word 'contract' into contradiction with its meaning. Plainly, when the word 'agreement' comes into being there should be parties who are consenting to the stipulated clauses. But there is no consent solicited from the black when the colonial contract is drafted and ratified. What comes to crush the black is the blow of colonial savagery.

Is there such a thing as a contract with regard to blacks? If there is, how is it contractual? The status of the colonial contract in relation to blackness has always been that of commandment. The contract is then a contradiction: it is an ontologically corrupt contract that legitimizes dispossession by conquest and the elimination of the life of the black.

The colonial contract, if it is insisted upon (as has been the case in colonial conquest), cannot assume its proper name of a contract. It cannot account for itself. It cannot justify itself, nor claim any form of legitimacy. These aforementioned problematics come into being because there is no contract in relation to the black. The ethical absence is the scandal: there is nothing ethical in the logic of conquest, despite colonialism's claim to have created an ethical contractual relation. However, the suppression of the scandal itself makes it impossible to account for. What exists is the persistent denial of the being of the black, and in propagating that denial the colonial contract is nothing but a fallacy. It is from this denial that the colonial contract authorizes itself without any form of accounting for what it is. As Sora Han (2015b) notes, it is a legal enforcement that perpetuates subjection. The black is not in any form of autonomous domain, but is bound by subjection and dispossessed of everything. This ontological crime, so gross and gruesome, petty and grand, baffling and unimaginable, does not, according to Frank Wilderson (2020), remain graspable in its scale and degree of abstraction. The colonial contract authorizes the congress of denial by propagating a narrative that nothing is done to the black, thereby absolving colonialism of its atrocities and continued machinations. Any language of claims, of being contractually contravened and defrauded, does not have standing. For Han (2015b, 396), this then demands making a case for these claims 'to be read and heard again'. But still, there is the instance of the non-juridical standing of the black. The black is nothing in terms of contractual standing, and there is nothing that, in the colonial contract, is extendable in fairness to be its 'terms' and 'conditions'. What is forever binding is everything that is against the black – say, dispossession. Not only is the black dispossessed, but whiteness deems blackness to be its own possession. Thus, there is no contractual relation between the possessor and the possessed. The possessed dispossessed is the double jeopardy of the black – subjection. This also means, according to Han (2015b, 397), that there is no determination of

22

'a contractual party by duress or consent'. Everything is under duress, and thus determining the contractual nature of things is futile; there is nothing in the contract that demands responsibility and having to extend forms of accounting.

As such, there is nothing that can be done to remedy this pathological condition that befalls the black, and it is the black who gets blamed for calamities brought upon itself. Things are the way they are. They should remain as they are. There is no need to change anything. So the prevailing view, the colonially racist one at that, is that it is better to leave the black behind as a distinct species of a different racial stock. This stock is seen as an ontological error created by the black. It cannot be corrected. The error is inscribed upon the black flesh in the form of a mark. There is no correction that can rectify the levels of distraction – the congress of denial's trick of inducing a form of forgetting – and destruction. There is damage without repair. There are shards, heaps of rubble, and a state of decay that signifies the rot that has eaten away the fibre of existence. The black, in the clauses of the colonial contract, is blamed for this state through pathologization. Everything about the black is defined along the lines of this pathologization as if it were ever natural.

The subject who is bound by the terms of the colonial contract is supposed to be a signatory to it. The endorsement of the colonial contract by law is to confirm that it is legal – that it is, above all else, a legal document. Enforced, enforceable and being the authorization of what is thus binding, the colonial contract is elaborated by the social order that forces the black into dispossession. The black is constructed to be outside the contract. The black is destroyed so as to be outside the contract. That is why the term 'colonial contract' comes to standardize the contract that has nothing to do with the black as a party to it. Its contractual terms have to do with the violation of the being of the black.

In a different formulation, but with the same disposition of course, Charles Mills (1997) refers to the 'Racial Contract'. As part of the continued violation of the black, it perpetrates the ruse of whiteness; it determines who gets what, and those who must get are whites. As Mills (1997, 9) states, 'the Racial Contract is an exploitation contract'. In the epistemological and ontological form of this contract, it is clear that things, including reality itself, are structured to preserve whiteness.

The authorizing signature

Contractual obligations come into being because there is an agreement. Two or more parties have entered into a contractual agreement. This means that there is a form of relation that is embodied by these signatories. The signed document will even serve as proof. Also, it will embody the details of such an agreement, and there will be terms and conditions that are not clearly apparent in the clauses. As soon as the signature is inscribed, when the document is marked, the document ceases to be what it is, and it becomes something else, a signed document – a contract. It is authorized and it is binding, and if it is to be dissolved there must be contractual terms to dissolve the system of relations.

The commandment of the law is what George Jackson (1972, 182) terms the 'oppressive contract', whose oppressive nature is evidenced by the legal standing of its signature. For there to be a signature there should be a document. The document has authenticity because the signature authorizes it. So, everything has legal standing. To sign is to mark and make. It is to render permanent, authorized and even legal what has been signed. It is to give the document some power to have legal standing and therefore to be binding. For the fact that the colonial contract is an agreement that is enforceable by law – in written or spoken form – as a structured commitment, undertaking, bond, settlement, arrangement, covenant and treaty means that it has binding force on the parties who are signatories to it. There is a form of relation, and it formalizes this relation as a signed agreement. The signature signifies a line, mark, inscription, originality, authority, legitimacy, authenticity, representation, truth.

As an authorizing inscription that materializes the object, the signature is inseparable from the power of the document as a complete form of writing. It is a final(ized) document. It expresses terms and conditions that bracket the absurdity of its clauses. At the same time, it expresses itself clearly or obscurely by stipulation. Read aloud, these stipulations are textual expressions, referred from the text. This, according to Jacques Derrida (1976, 141), is a 'language with a complete writing' which turns out to be 'also a law of language'. This language, that of the law in the absolute sense, the law that commands, that is to say subjection, elaborates the power of the colonial regime as the writing of the absolute. The law, the base and supplement of the colonial contract, causes the black to stand outside any form of ontological (re)presentation. Since everything is against the black, that being the structure of reality as such – antiblackness – the black's everyday life does not become habitable and is mere survival. Everything that has to do with the elaboration of life can be dispossessed at will. The black is subjected to the excess of language that comes with the clauses of the colonial contract.

This contract is not there to be read and interpreted by the black. It is not a contract for the black. The colonial contract, with its violent ramifications, which are obviously antiblack, unfolds as a matter of surprise due to the excessive nature of its absurd clauses. By its intentions and purposes, the colonial contract qua law is the solidification of 'the racial order of the *socius*' (Han 2015a, 40). Its clauses speak the language of subjection. It is the law that has language, above language – simply put, it is the language itself, metalanguage. The colonial contract embodies this violent language. The law is there to legitimize this language by appropriating it and expressing it in the way the contractual clauses are stipulated. The impassioned language of law makes sure that it stands erect as a command. It must be absolute and clinically clear; it cannot be speculative, uncertain, reflexive, convoluted. Calvin Warren (2018, 67) is correct in stating that 'the law is an ontological instrument'. According to Warren, the law is there to conceal the ontological terror of the colonial contract. The colonial contract appears as simple as possible because it is a commandment. The manner in which it is structured as a chain of supplements means that it is 'an intact purity to both the negative and the positive' (Derrida 1976, 246). The axis of the negative and the positive is not only the binary of the interior and exterior. It also assumes the state of contradiction by being situated at both poles. That is to say, the colonial contract gets discharged with unfolding contradictions, and should they compromise the colonial interests they will be repealed and amended at will. The poles of negative and positive assume a place in the interior and the exterior through supplementary means.

By being a literal form, the colonial contract claims to be original by the very fact of being embedded in its colonial origin. It must be a clear text that is taken as the origin of not only language, but reality itself. The literal inscription of the colonial contract means that it is not metaphorical. If it contains absurd clauses (which is often the case), its literal meaning is final. 'Then, the literal or proper meaning will be the relationship of the idea to the affect it *expresses*' (Derrida 1976, 278, emphasis in the original). The imprisoned language, its spirit, its embodied expression, makes it possible for the commandment to be authorized. The expressive affect, by means of a declarative text that is absolute and enclosed, is the reality that gets drilled into the head of the black who is at the receiving end of colonial conquest. Even if some clauses might be seductive, the materialization of clear expression of the colonial contract makes it the power that binds.

The law as the colonial contract

But then, why is the law still needed to enforce the colonial contract? Is it not enough to stop at the view that the colonial contract exists in the colonial regime? What about the law itself? Is the law not a structure that enforces subjection? The terms in which the colonial contract is drawn up, and it being filled with the clauses of impassioned language, its spirit being colonially embodied, why can it not be a colonial inscription? Is the colonial contract independent of colonialism? There is no difference between them; in fact, the two are embodied in the very thing that defends colonialism. This law is the colonial contract itself in so far as its jurisprudence is concerned. The spirit of the law, its lettered spirit, is colonial and it is a form of automatic writing that is invested in legitimizing colonial conquest. Giorgio Agamben (1998, 52) counsels thus: 'For life under a law that is in force without signifying resembles life in the state of exception, in which the most innocent gestures or the smallest forgetfulness can have most extreme consequences'. The black is under siege. The black is the figure of the outlaw. The law, in its unlawful acts, still wants to maintain its status of being beyond approach. It is, in its spirit, the tongue of the law, what Han (2015a, 4) calls the 'stubborn paradox', which is fundamentally antiblack and refuses any form of contradiction. The utterability of the colonial word, the reading aloud of the colonial contract, demands nothing from the black but stupefied silence. The black is to be violated endlessly with the absurd view that there should be no resistance. With the colonial contract in hand, colonial conquest wields power that can be exercised at will because it is designed to go unchecked. This sadistic paradigm derives its source from the acts of citationality, which Han (2015a, 3) refers to as the 'law's citational world' – say, what creates a 'legal devotion' – the law as the arresting practice and the colonial contract as the legal text. Here, there is a suspension of anything and everything ethical, and what reigns is what Fred Moten (2018b, 247) calls 'an ethics of the obscene'. For, in so far as the black is concerned, there are no ethical dilemmas that can be entertained in relation to the black (Wilderson 2010). There is no accounting needed because the law (which is lawless) cannot subject itself to account for its despotic excess. This despotic excess is also the law – say, the blurring of the legal and extra-legal. It is the law that commands obedience. It is the law of laws. It is the law that is above the law. It is the universal law. *It is the law.* Immune from anything. Accounting for nothing. Being absolute. Unlimited, to put it plainly. In Derrida's words (2018, 35), 'the law as such, apparently, should never give rise to any narrative. In order to be invested with its categorical authority, the law should have no history, no genesis, no derivation whatever. That would be the law of law'.

How can things be legal in the greater scheme of illegality? How can illegality stand as the paragon of legality? So is the world as it stands, so is its reality (having been elaborated through propagation of falsity until it becomes truth). Colonial conquest is an ontological crime. It is unleashed in such a manner that its arbitrary nature is overly stretched, without limits, and no line is drawn for how far things can go. Blacks are positioned to be at the receiving end of despotic terror. It is this form of ontological destruction that is unleashed without conceding.

By exercise of power, by subjection that is, this writing embodies what Derrida (1976, 157) calls a 'chain of supplements' to elaborate what is not there with what is there: 'the play of substitution fills and marks a determined lack'. The colonial contract is not a substitution, but the elaborate intensification of falsity with the aim of absoluteness. The writing process that comes into the drafting of the colonial contract has been nothing but the elimination of the life of the black. Nothing is there to defend and endorse the black. The black has nothing in the condition that dispossesses. The violence that authorizes the colonial contract is the destructive force, and its eliminationist logic that is driven by genocidal impulses means that the law cannot be held accountable to checks and balances. These checks and balances give the illusion that the law is impartial. This is nothing but liberal deceit.

The law is legally enforceable, it is obligatory, and in the colonial regime, it is a commandment, the *coerced obligation*. Sylvia Wynter (1994, 43) calls this a 'universe of obligations' where the colonial contract is imposed on the black. The writing that is contained in it (its clauses) has no sense of relation which is extendable to blacks. Jackson (1972, 182) has this to say: 'History is clearly a long continuum of synthesizing elements. The imbalances of the oppressive contract, ideas so fundamentally contradictory, and forces so mutually exclusive can only result in the dissolution of the agents of that contradiction'. And furthermore, 'the corollary of the contract is quite simply malignancy. It strikes first in the region of the brain. A search for a nondiseased mind throws one hard against one of the greatest historical/biological calamities imaginable' (Jackson 1972, 182). There is a colonial contract; it is colonial neurosis. Foremost among the effects of this contract is the fact that the black is made vulnerable to the fantasies that come with the ontological violence which makes the black an object, a dehumanized thing.

With the power that comes with colonial conquest, its weight on blacks, what Anthony Farley (2003, 690) calls 'masters-over-slaves', there is a system of superiority of whites and inferiority of blacks that denotes the infrastructure of violence which dictates who is human and who is not. All this is based on the logic of racism. If blacks are erased from the realm of the human, so is their subjectivity. Whatever they think, feel and do does not matter.

The absence of consent is the mark of tragedy. Édouard Glissant (1997, 52) corroborates this argument thus: 'Tragedy springs from any situation in which community consent is threatened'. Colonial conquest, with the colonial contract in hand, threatens the community and destroys it through invasion and dispossession; its actualization comes to be witnessed through the manner in which tragedy is unleashed. Its source is nothing internal, but rather something external that is perpetually manufactured to serve as the very fibre of that community. The community is atomised in order to fragment whatever exists within it that might serve as its knotted bond. Consent then becomes immaterial, because racialized violence has already been kickstarted, with the black as its target. How can consent be sought in the colonial contract? Tragedy is what marks this reality.

In Western thought, in its world, says Glissant (1997, 47), there is a hidden cause, and what is prevalent is 'a project' that comes into being in terms of how time is configured. Tellingly, this linear and hidden cause is, in all ways, that of tragedy: 'The tragic action is the uncovering of what has gone unnoticed' (1997, 52). Even Glissant's 'poetics of relation' cannot capture the tragedy that is discharged by colonial conquest and its destructive elements that make rubble out of black bodies. Here is the antithesis of any form of relation, the truth about the colonial contract itself:

> The totalitarian is introduced in relation on the basis of
> some nonprime element (violence, for example, or race)

whose definition is overdetermined but knowledge of which, nonetheless, has limits. This totalitarian relation is, in turn, approachable, but its definition cannot be imagined. Because one cannot imagine a relation – open – among elements the knowledge of which has boundaries. Totality, on the other hand, like Relation, is not approached, but its definition is imaginable. (Glissant 1997, 171)

There is nothing but foreclosure in the terms of the colonial contract. Relation necessitates contact which, paradoxically, is the aberration in the colonial contract since the black, as the figure of nothing, cannot enter into any form of contractual relation. The black is thus fixed as the figure of transgression. The colonial contract then assumes the status of a disciplinary tool; hence its immunity from being subjected to critique and outright rejection. The protection that the colonial contract has is not the protection of the document. It is not, say, a sacred text which must be immune from potential blasphemous utterances and inscriptions. The mask of violence, the colonial regime legitimizing its racist fantasies and thus executing violence on scales of magnitude, erects and solidifies immunity as a way of disempowering the black in order to make subjection a way of life. That is why the colonial contract can be said to be the condemnation and damnation of the black. That is why the signatories of the colonial contract are whites, and their whiteness is not positioned as a set of interests but as existence itself, which must be structured according to the logic of antiblackness. The reality of being subjected to death and being contractually abstracted (which is legally enforced and legitimized), the calculus of existence that relegates the black to zero – the sucking of life from the black to the point of absolute depletion – demonstrates the capacity of the law (in its general provisions, application and administration) to justify the killability of the black.

Two things: the black is always folded, enclosed and saturated by investment in liberal conformism, after having been excluded and crushed out of subjecthood through dispossession that is enabled by the excess of the colonial contract. And the black is bound by the colonial contract while having no claim to its provisions (of course, there cannot be such claims since the contract is antiblack), and not being a signatory to it. Still, to ponder the fallacy of the colonial contract, or to contest whether it is a contract or not, seems to be futile.

The politics of the colonial contract

The colonial contract comes with chemical and mechanical forces that construct the black body as a thing. As Saidiya Hartman (1997) rightfully states, this is the production of the black body as the aberration, a thing. Then, what emerges is the form of politics that informs the colonial contract, what Hartman (1997, 59) terms 'anatomo-politics', which are invested in the ontological destruction of the black. These are politics that drive the actualization of colonial fantasies contained in the clauses of the colonial contract. The anatomo-politics decree that the ontological disenfranchisement of the black be instituted. Thus, there should not be any point of contact with blacks. Politics have to do with civility (thus the extension, folding and constituting of the trinitarian embodiment of liberty, equality and justice); these do not extend to the black. The anatomo-politics expel the black from subjecthood. By this means of depersonalization, the black is structurally prejudiced (everything is against the black). 'Yet if the law cannot change prejudice, its role is to affirm it?' asks Hartman (1997, 192). The answer to this question is the affirmative stance, a pointed *yes*. The stigmatizing character of anatomo-politics makes the ontological violence directed at the black legal. As such, the black is not backed by any legal institution. There are no legal remedies that are due to the black; the law is against the black because it endorses the colonial contract. In contractual terms, there is no breach against the black at all. The law is claimed to be innocent; it is immune from being charged by being responsible for affirming the colonial contract and the prejudicial character that unleashes ontological destruction on the black. The status of the law, when it comes to the black, is that of utter absence. There is law as the affirmative structure that is just for all humans, but in reality not for the ontologically erased black. The black and the law are rendered absolutely separate in ontological terms. This ontological difference, and its basis for separation, makes it impossible for the black to make contractual claims. As Hartman (1997, 195) says, 'furthermore, the exclusivity of whiteness was identified as the essential ingredient in reproducing black degradation'. For the colonial contract is the content and concrete form of whiteness.

The black exists within the paradox of construction and destruction. What is constructed by the racist infrastructure is the very thing that serves as the destruction of the black. What is destroyed by this infrastructure is that which should serve as the black's vitality. The place of the black remains irresolvable in terms of what is at stake. There is war against the black. It is war against those who do not legally abide. The systemic warfare that is directed towards the black is, in many ways, ontological destruction. Everything is against the black, who is the aberration from the norm, the criminal in the face of the law and the pathological in the face of existence. The law authorizes the elimination of the black, which is sanctioned by law without any form of recourse because the black bears criminality. Therefore, the verdict is predictably and always guilty, guilty, guilty. Even the taking away of life from blacks happens through the institution of the law. The killability of black life is present in the laws that are there to facilitate death.

The position of the black

What is prescribed in the colonial contract is a violent inscription – the pronouncement to the black that 'the wrath shall fall upon thee' – that the black will be burdened, crushed and left to be nothing. These are the contractual terms and conditions. It is permissible, therefore, for the colonial contract to issue a plethora of decrees and interdicts (permanently, so without relief, as a binding force even) against the black. Indeed, this is allowed, willed and encouraged.

The black is always, at the level of speech, interdicted. This is the castration of black speech in the face of the violent markings of the colonial contract. In taking the antagonistic position that is necessary to wage an existential struggle by rendering the colonial contract a crisis, the black must call for a crisis and for what Wilderson (2003a, 225) calls the elaboration of 'a theory of crisis', which is key in exposing the genocidal impulses that engender the tragedy of the black. Wilderson (2003a, 225) argues that by elaborating the antagonistic position, the expression of the grammar of the black with its insatiable demands, in order to struggle to exist in the face of dehumanization, the black must emerge as 'the unthought' to render the current order of things, as underwritten by the colonial contract, a scandal. The antagonistic position is then to destabilize the status quo.

As aforementioned, there is no way there can be a contract in the condition of invasion, destruction and death. There cannot be any form of agreement in this structured ontological violation. There is no agreement in what is unilateral; but bilateral and multilateral contractual modes are not spared from being colonial. Agreement can accentuate the colonial contract. But worth underlining is the fact that the colonial contract is filled with the spirit of commandments and does not allow any agreement. Therefore, to say 'the colonial contract' is to say asymmetry, non-relation, subjection. But then, something needs to be said about the contract and contact. This is important in illuminating what happens when the black is placed in this fold. The black moves through and is moved through structures as constraints and prohibitions that necessitate ontological violence.

Since relation in the colonial contract is an oxymoron, it is from the tearing down of the colonial contract that relation might emerge or be figured out, after it has been forged, genuinely so. The colonial condition is a violent one. After the colonial contract has been torn apart, after the colonial condition has been subjected to continued existential struggle (antagonism and not negotiation), then, for the black, there can be what might be termed *a better world*.

By assuming the antagonistic position, the figure of the black is not in a position to engage in debates about the problematic clauses of the colonial contract. Rather, the position is that of tearing up the colonial contract altogether. In fact, the concern is not about the colonial contract per se, but about the ending of the world that makes the colonial contract exist in the first place. This different order of questions is presented by Wilderson (2003a), and does not concern any form of soliciting reparative gestures. The discursive registers of the black are grounded in the grammar of suffering, the incoherent grammar which cannot be articulated by the black; they exist in the face of the 'assumptive logic' of what Wilderson (2003a, 225) terms 'private initiatives' under the command of the hegemonic situation of antiblackness, which cannot grasp the insatiable demands put forth by the black. As such, there can be no discourse in that there is no civic platform or public forum for it, because what the black elaborates is not issues for debate but matters of life and death that are caused and ignored by the private initiatives of antiblackness.

The signature of the colonial contract is the authorization of death. By manufacturing and producing this ontological ruin, the contract ensures that death will be pervasive in a way that is seen not as barbarity but as civility. Ontological violence is legitimized through hegemonic practices that propagate a singularity which serves as the dominant narrative licensing the death of the black, without any form of accounting. The suspension of humanity is the ontological dispossession that has structurally marked the black. This violence happens in ways that defy any narrative. It exists in the realm of the unasked questions. The death project is licensed by the colonial contract. The idea of conquest (under the guise of civilization) is propagated as if it did not, does not and will not leave heaps and heaps of corpses, which are regarded as merely things through the fact of being black. According to this logic, no one has died. The singular narrative gets peddled that nothing was done to the black. All that was done was preserving the common ideal, the common good. Everything that is seen as standing in the way of civilization must be 'dealt with' to fast-track the process of civilization, to make the world a better place, and for everyone. The race against time to build a better world has happened at the ontological expense of the black. This civilization has been nothing but the ontological extraction of the black. The black is subjected to the colonial condition in the name of 'building' a civilization. The black, the obstacle, has to be 'dealt with'. The black as the obstruction is the fiction that is actualized to mask the invasion, conquest, destruction, and the elevation of genocidal impulses when killing is just the itemized object of the death project – the killing of the black for the sake of killing.

Blackness is locatable. It is the black; it is what the black is. The black of blackness is the articulation of being. The curatorial site of blackness, for the black to be healed from the infrastructure of violence, even caring for itself, will not originate from any form of contractual formulation. The colonial contract resides in forms and arrangements that have nothing to do with the literality of the concept 'contract' in that the ontological violence against the black should be justified. The black is not there. What happened to the black did not happen because there is nothing there. If there is something that happened to blacks, it is nothing. There is nothing that can be done to what is not there. Therefore, the exoneration of whiteness, and its impulsive denial of its responsibility to abate antiblackness, is what makes it illegitimate for blacks to make a claim that they have been and continue to be wronged.

There is, in so far as the black is concerned, only the non-contractual. What can be deemed to be political sentiments, what comes with being the bearer of rights, the legal subject, one who has standing in relation to the contract, is 'the freedom of contract', which for Han (2015b, 399) is the realm of exchange of contractual subjects who accept terms and conditions that have nothing to do with the black. The colonial contract is couched in unambiguous terms that eliminate contradictions. It aims to 'promote a voluntarist theory of enslavement' (Han 2015b, 401). There is nothing transparent in it, everything is concealed. The colonial contract is the colonial darkest secret.

The colonial contract is a 'death project', in Julia Suárez-Krabbe's precise formulation (Suárez-Krabbe 2016, 3). The death project, as legitimized by the colonial contract, structurally absolves all the ontological crimes that are committed against the black. Nothing was done to the black. Nothing happened. What actually happened is nothing. So, nothing can be done to or about what is nothing. The black, who is nothing in the colonial scheme of things, cannot claim anything that was done or is done. There is just nothing. Nothing at all. With this logic of ontological erasure, the violent inscription of the colonial infrastructure in both the consciousness and unconsciousness of whiteness, the licensing of the death project by the colonial contract, causes the black not to be there.

For the death project to have this indexing effect, clearly there is no contractual standing of any form to be vouched for. For it, just as for its parallel – the colonial contract – there is contractual nothingness. Suffice it to say that the death project, by way of definition, 'refers to the exercise of violence in colo-niality, which targets the actual process of life and conditions of existence: in short, plurality' (Suárez-Krabbe 2016, 3). The singularity of the death project resides in its dehumanization and predictable execution of death. What is life is made into a form of scarcity. Survival becomes instituted as the mode of existence.

The position of the black, the antagonistic one, comprises demands that cannot be satisfied. The colonial contract is formed in the infrastructure of conquest and it is here that there is no space for the discursive engagement of the black. The consent that is extended to the black is a false gesture. It is, in a way, the structural denial of the black *tout court*! The form of violence that comes with the colonial contract is, according to Wilderson (2003a), the one that kills, as it is gratuitous. The colonial contract is instituted to 'serve as the vehicle of white self-exploitation, renunciation, and enjoyment' (Hartman 1997, 26). This is done through the ontological violence that is directed towards the black body. That which is identifiably relegated to the black is rendered fungible, which, for Hartman, means being rendered abstract and immaterial – the very absence of onto-logical status. The black is made available and vulnerable to be consumed and disposed of by this violence. This is the violence that is warranted by the clauses of the colonial contract, 'its hyper-discursive violence that kills the black subject that the concept, civil society, may live' (Wilderson 2003a, 231).

In a certain sense, the black has been the tearing up of the colonial contract. No one agrees to be subjected to subjection. The black stands in the name of resistance. This is clear in the position of antagonism. It is out, out there – *exteriori*. It is the open, openness – the resistance which is the break from the inside and closure. The black is embodied in the spirit called blackness. Wynter (1994), in confronting the colonial contract, calls for rewriting the episteme. This is done on terms that are dictated by the black. It is the black *in-itself* as opposed to being represented, and thus outsourcing its means of freedom.

The figure of the black is, by way of Nahum Chandler (2014), a problem for thought, it being racialized as a problem and being the agent that problematizes the way it has been racialized. The epistemic unfolding, which is tied to the idea of the political – the existential struggle as the locus of the black – is the prob-lematization of reality as it is (antiblackness), and this is a way of re-(con)figuration of the ways of being. Drawing on what Wynter (1994) refers to as the order of rewriting the episteme, Chandler says that the black is the itinerary, and by assertion, the locus where 'the thought of possibility of the other, in its apparent simplicity, should suffice' (Chandler 2014, 70). This is possible in the ways of unthinking the colonial contract, which means situating it in the right place – the realm of the non-contractual. The 'racial distinction' that Chandler (2014, 34) points to is assigned and relegated to what enunciates the protocols that tear up the colonial contract, that is, where the ensemble of questions ruptures the contract. This, in line with Wynter's protocol of rewriting the episteme, takes the form of what Chandler triply frames as the problem, problematic and problematization. What he solicits is put thus:

> If one would mark the force inscribing the first historical experience of (racialized) violence by the name the force of the double, then that force which inscribes the second historical experience of (racialized) violence is what may be remarked as the double force of the force of the double. (Chandler 2014, 107)

The colonial contract is the problematic in Chandler's meditations. What Chandler (2014, 107) emphasizes is 'the strange and powerful play of a certain asymmetry and symmetry'. This is the structure of reality that the colonial contract imposes. To contend with this structural arrangement of ontological violence, there needs to be a radical way in which the colonial contract is exposed as racialized violence. The racial distinction that the black is thrown into is a way of writing this figure outside life. Therefore, the colonial inscription that underpins the colonial conquest, and which claims to be the sole system of thought (colonialists with a singular narrative), effects a contract that is binding. The resistance against the colonial contract always marks a beginning. This is a beginning which does not claim to be a path towards a telos. It is a beginning of what Chandler sees as the figure of the rupture and the emergent, a site where possibilities are propelled to problematize the problematic of the colonial contract. This is the inauguration of 'the general pathways by which subjectivation and the bearing of historical process unfolds' (Chandler 2014, 169). This is the site where the problem of thought is illuminated.

Furthermore, this is the critical practice that sees the config-uration of knowledge (the colonial contract being the primary site of it) as the organization of power that must be subjected to antagonisms. The ethical attitude comes into being as an emer-gent of the problematic, the black as the enunciator of critique, where the colonial contract is problematized from its source of power. This is what Chandler (2014) amplifies as the structure of a viewpoint. It is the viewpoint that sees the world from the locus of the black. This way of seeing, where thought is illumi-nated, comes to be called the position of the unthought (Hartman and Wilderson 2003). When problems emerge from those who are being denied their humanity the terms of discourse change. Lewis Gordon (2000) is right to state that ethical questions come from people who are not a problem, but people with problems. These problems are structured in such a way that the black is ontologically corrupted by the infrastructure of racism not to see itself from its own point of view. It is in assuming the struc-ture of a viewpoint that the black, by way of problematization, poses fundamental questions that confront colonial conquest and its resultant colonial contract. The rupture ensues, and its beginning foregrounds and charts the trajectory of the epistemic unfolding that illuminates ideas that will chisel at the epistemic closure. This closure cannot cement itself by claiming to be universal while it is a particularity that has been shielding, and masked by, whiteness under the guise of universalism.

This will only come about through the spearheading of what Wynter (1994, 69) calls 'the speech of a new frontier of knowledge' – the register that unlearns by rigorously tearing apart the colonial contract and not bothering to (re)negotiate it. This is, indeed, a disagreement, a decisive point of antago-nism. The black does not agree to the colonial contract. Even though the black is criminalized, and the spirit of blackness is demonized, the existential struggle ensues relentlessly to tear up the colonial contract. The antiblack structure that is ratified as the actualized reality of the world is exposed by the black: the sense in which precarity entangles blackness, and consigns it to the status of dehumanization that is mechanized, operationalized and weaponized to make the black into a thing (thus violently collapsing the status of human as a way of ontological erasure). This is the justification of intensified ontological violence as a statement of fact, of the state of affairs – reality as it is – as the unalterable thing about which nothing can be done. The black survives through claiming the right to live even though this life is denied. Therefore, the colonial order of things is fiercely opposed through the spirit of blackness. Blackness continues to act and confront the crushing weight that comes with the colonial contract.

To conclude, it is necessary to unearth the racist underpinnings and unmake the racist pretensions that come in the name of the law, which is the legitimizing force of the colonial contract and the colonial project writ large. Clearly, what arises from the discursive protocols of blackness is the colonial contract; that is the ontological scandal. For the black, there is nothing contractual in so far as the colonial contract is concerned. This, in fact, facilitates the attitudinal stance of blackness, which does not contest the clauses of the colonial contract but rejects it as a whole, and thus roots this rejection in the existential struggle that combats antiblackness.

The birth of Azania is what dislodges the colonial contract. If there is to be a rebirth of the nation, that cannot happen according to the logics of settler-colonialism and its continued effects. Azania, contra the colonial contract, is what is yet to come, not in terms of the name of the country only but in regard to what overhauls the whole edifice of settler-colonialism. That, as a matter of fact, does not happen within the framework of liberal democracy that underwrites post-1994 South Africa – a framework which, in itself, is a dismal failure in dealing with the problem of antiblackness. Instead, since there can be no colonial contract, or any contract for that matter, written outside the black, what must emerge is a set of conditions of possibility for reimagining the logos and ethos of liberation.

Azania is a different reality that is brought by the black. Since this is the land of the free, and not apologetic for settler-colonialism and its logics, it is another reality that will emerge from the black point of view. If Azania emerges by renaming the country, while the black continues to experience the symptomatic deliriums of settler-colonialism, thus perpetuating it with a black face in command of things, that will not at all be liberation. It will mean that the colonial contract is still in place. So, Azania will mean the tearing up of the colonial contract and not the rewriting of it. What is yet to be written is liberation.

2 | On Land and Being

The land question will forever remain the ontological scandal and its modes of disavowal will reach a point of exhaustion.

The land question remains a question in that the answer to it is often avoided. There has been a plethora of interventions on the land question, but there is political paralysis in dealing with the question that squarely confronts the land question, let alone with the fact that the conception of being – the ontological entity so to speak – is rendered absent, if not erased, from the land question. The absence of being suggests that the importance of land has nothing to do with those to whom land is of paramount importance. Added to that, the story of antiblack racism is a continuing silence. This means that there is no race in the land question; the land question is a question with no racist-settler-colonial past and its aftermath.

The origin of the land question

The origin of the land question can be located in the historical scandal of the racist-settler-colonial arrangement that stretches as far back as the colonial encounter of 1652. Thami ka Plaatjie (2003, 287) argues that 'the land crisis in this country dates back to 1652, when the first white settlers arrived to stay in the country and commenced dispossessing Africans of their land'. The Natives Land Act (No. 27 of 1913) is not the beginning of land dispossession as the post-1994 land discourse seems to suggest, but rather a continuation of the racist-settler-colonial land theft that was inaugurated in 1652. The difference, of course, is that the Natives Land Act legalized land theft and institutionalized, naturalized and normalized the existential condition of landlessness of the black. It is still unimaginable, according to Wellington Thwala (2002, 2), that the 'Native[s] Land Act resulted in only 10 per cent of the land [being] reserved for blacks'. According to Lungisile Ntsebeza (2005, 2–3), this was notorious legislation that 'appropriated more than 90 per cent of the land surface'. As a result, white farmers benefited from substantial farming subsidies, while black agriculture was constrained and depleted. This was followed by the passing of the Native Trust and Land Act (No. 18 of 1936), which allocated the already promised land to the reserves (the areas geographically marked for black people, who did not have the right to own property there). What also followed was the Native Laws Amendment Act (No. 46 of 1937), which prevented blacks from buying land in the urban areas.

The land question (re)produced white privilege and black dispossession. It is clear from those draconian colonial laws that the life of the black was meant to be made difficult, and the condition of being landless was legally entrenched to the existential point of seeming like a matter of common sense. In short, it was good and well for the black to be landless. If the land question is raised, more so in the post-1994 period, this will disturb the order of liberal democracy which, in itself, has no interest in addressing the land question.

It is worth noting that, with the advent of apartheid, the misery of land dispossession was intensified by the passing of the Group Areas Act (No. 41 of 1950), which forced blacks to live on small areas of land that were dysfunctional in terms of commercial activity. The period of the 1950s saw the aggression towards land dispossession being hyper-legalized through the passing of the Group Areas Act, the Bantu Authorities Act (No. 68 of 1951), and the Promotion of Bantu Self-Government Act (No. 46 of 1959). It cannot be denied that this existential misery is violence par excellence, and it is a historical scandal that cannot be sanitized, denied, or erased. If the conception of being of the black is to be taken seriously, its ontological presence should be understood as liminal, as it is still haunted by settler-colonialism. This is the history of dehumanization, which logically means that there is a need for reparations, more so if the promise of the 1994 settlement was termed 'liberation'. But this was not the case, of course. The promise turned into a betrayal. Andile Mngxitama challenges this narrative, arguing as follows:

> The South African social, political and economic realities of today are founded on the long colonial conquest and, later, apartheid land dispossessions, oppression and exploitation of Africans. Imbedded in these is the race issue linked to the objectives of Rhodes and his predecessors, later perfected by crude apartheid ideologues into a policy of racially based accumulation and control. (Mngxitama 2006, 41)

The market as the post-1994 policy framework

The nature of the land question in the post-1994 South African state is marked by the legacy of land dispossession, which demands reparative justice and accounting. Such demands are the cries to give the land to the landless – that is, 'returning the land to its rightful owners – the indigenous people of South

Africa' (Ka Plaatjie 2003, 288). The African National Congress assumed power in 1994 and committed itself to making the land question its major priority, and to fulfilling the expectations of blacks who have been landless throughout centuries of racist-settler-colonial domination. Land reform was part of the agenda of the African National Congress in order to realize transformation, but it fell short with the adoption of neo-liberal policies. Since the promise was made to give the land to the landless, ineffective policies have been put in place. According to Ruth Hall (2009), government initiatives relating to land reform do not translate into tangible transformation. Mngxitama (2001) further contends that though land policies can appear to be impressive projects, there is little reason to suggest that land reform has been effective.

It is common knowledge that the land reform policies of South Africa have been liberally lifted from the neo-liberal and restrictive policy frameworks of the World Bank reports on land reform and its pretentious boast of 'development'. This means that there is no original blueprint of land reform and, accordingly, this makes it impossible for there to be viable land reform since all policy initiatives are trapped within frameworks governed by the principle of the market. These policy frameworks entail that the status quo should remain, and that they should be linked to performance in the marketplace, as transferring land without this linkage would destroy the economy.

What is often evoked is the question of the market, and it is argued that the workings of the market must not be disrupted, so as to create conditions whereby livelihoods are sustained. The logic of the market essentially entails 'business as usual', because it is a site of certainty in the face of uncertainty. The previous patterns of land ownership, use and production should thus continue as they were, and not be interrupted. This implies that those who own land are putting it to good use; they are, in many ways, benefiting the economic standing of the country, and they are also feeding the nation. With this broad stroke of a brush, the market – and not being – is made the very important bedrock on which the land question should be sanitized, and also apparently 'resolved'. This means that it is through blind faith in the market, and leaving it to its own devices, that the land question has resolved itself. According to the logic of the market, there is no land question at all but just some economic imbalances that have to do with access or lack thereof in the marketplace.

So, there is no question of historical land theft, a glaring crime perpetrated by settler-colonialists which still benefits whites to this day. This idea is solidified by the climate of political correctness in the land discourse and the moralistic posture of a country that claims to have no violent past, just a past that people should transcend in order to build a better future. If there is such a silence about the past, why is there so much emphasis on the present and the future? Even the logic of the market has a past to it, and it is not as if the market has been serving the best interests of those who have been violated by the past. The landless black has been the figure excluded from the market, and this has been hyper-legalized. The market in the present perpetuates the very same violations as in the past, and (re)produces the plague of land dispossession and superfluity of blackness.

It is the market that is used as a device to bar those who are dispossessed of land from having any form of livelihood. There should be no land question qua being, but rather land qua market. It is the latter which invites the euphemisms of economic stability, competitiveness, human security, food security and 'feeding the nation'. These are mere rhetorical devices that have nothing to do with justice and reparations. The market is the sole determinant of the political ontology, and the livelihood of the nation must gravitate towards the market. To criticize the market means to be irrational.

The interesting thing about the logic of the market is that it is a neo-liberal construct that buttresses the historical scandal of being that the land question must still address. The caveat within this logic is that the politics of pragmatism must take precedence. The market should precede the state, and even be outside it, to legitimize the arability and commodification of land. It is the mantra of neo-liberalism that everything should be left to the dictates of the market. Even if landlessness is the perennial question of the day in post-1994 South Africa, this question loses its potency as everything is subsumed by the market. What is interesting in South Africa is that the state has been a major player in this regard – that is, in seeing the land as a commodity through which the economy can flourish. The neo-liberal ideology of the South African state means that it has faith in the market, and there is no agency at all to account for the land question.

The land question and the South African Constitution

The South African Constitution (Republic of South Africa 1996) is lauded as the 'highest law of the land'. This suggests that the Constitution is the embodiment of the nation, aligned with the politics of goodwill. In terms of the land question, the Constitution is an arbiter. What is contended here is that assuming such a position means that the historical scandal of the land question cannot be rectified within the ambit of the Constitution, which is itself a constraint on doing so. This means there is no possibility of restoring land by righting the wrongs of the colonial past and their continued presence. The Constitution is part of the current discursive order inaugurated by the negotiated settlement which brought about the post-1994 South Africa, where the land question has not been confronted but has been trivialized as something that is complex and yet impossible to resolve. Yet there was enough purpose in the negotiations to give a constitutional guarantee to the settler-colonial arrangement through a property clause. This means the latter is the order of things, and creates the impression that it is in the interest of everyone.

The property clause – Section 25 of the Constitution – is the basis of how the land question is intended to be resolved. This clause, in the first instance, recognizes the right to own private property. Secondly, it recognizes the state's responsibility to introduce land reform, implying that the right to property cannot prevent land reform. Thirdly, it stipulates that land reform includes the use of expropriation of property in the general interest. Ntsebeza (2005) is of the view that the property clause in the Constitution is the major obstacle to large-scale land reform. This clause is constitutionally entrenched, and it prevents any form of challenge. The protection of the property clause seems to suggest that land theft is legislatively justified. It is also Ntsebeza's contention that it is not possible to redress past injustices while the existing property rights are recognized and entrenched. In amplification, Ka Plaatjie writes:

> The consistent use of the rule of law as a means of stalling the land reform process is a critical stumbling block for the acceleration of the restitution process. The farmers raise the issue of legal title to ownership as an indisputable basis for continued ownership. What is not raised is the violent manner in which land was initially acquired. The current crisis on the farms in South Africa is partially a reflection of this reality. (Ka Plaatjie 2003, 306)

51

Truly, there is the absence of being in this clause, and no mention is made of the settler-colonialism through which the land question was created. This is the very clause that is said to complicate the issue of land reform, in that it somehow recognizes the land rights acquired through colonialism and apartheid (Hall 2003; Mngxitama 2001; Ntsebeza 2005, 2007). This clause still legitimizes protection of the land that was stolen and fails to account for landlessness. Mngxitama (2004) argues that the very basis of the clause is the aim to boost foreign direct investment, which means that continued land dispossession is removed from the equation. Rather, the emphasis of the clause is that it is in line with the international standards set by the United Nations on ensuring equal access to property (South African Human Rights Commission 2003). Yet there can never be equal access to property while the conception of being and landlessness is not directly addressed.

This solidifies a form of neo-liberal guarantee whereby those who benefited from the violent land theft by racist-settler-colonialists will be expediently safeguarded at the expense of those racialized blacks who are in the ontological realm of land dispossession. The Constitution eliminates the conception of being from the land question. It makes no mention of race or antiblack racism in so far as the land question is concerned. This absence of race is the absence of being. Thus, it is imperative, according to this dominant narrative, to make sure that the land question stands alone as a floating signifier with no relation to ontological questions. What is clear is that if the land question is closely tied to the ontological conception of being, it cannot be resolved through the Constitution because the latter does not cater for such a conception; the land question is an extra-constitutional issue if the conception of being is the fulcrum of this question. The Constitution has nothing to do with the land question other than to constrain its resolution. The colonial question of land dispossession stemming from the 1652 colonial encounter is not touched upon by the Constitution, let alone a direct confrontation with the 1913 Natives Land Act.

Those who are existentially wronged, the black landless, are not allowed to articulate their own demands regarding land as they have their own meaning for the land, different from the dominant narrative of post-1994 South Africa. Because they are ontologically dispossessed, they do not even have a right that gives them a form of constitutional access and privilege. Even the question of what land signifies to them is downplayed, if not subjected to total erasure and non-existence.

The Constitution is thus a neo-liberal device through which the land question is silenced in terms of addressing the funda-mental question of being. The land question is not a legal one in the sense of wanting a constitutional intervention. Its origin is the conception of violence that preceded the legislative inter-vention of the Natives Land Act. It arises from the politics of violence, and makes a legitimate claim that continued owner-ship that is racially white is in itself violence. This, of course, takes for granted that the systematic and systemic nature of white settler-colonialism is still the ontological scandal that acts through history. Therefore, being mute in regard to violence means that the Constitution is limited when it comes to the land question, in that it does not account for the conception of being that is landless.

What seems to be the embodiment of the Constitution with regard to the land question is nothing but silence; the neo-liberal eclipse of imagination cannot be a disappointment to those who have benefited from the history of violence. The foundational nature of the politics of appeasement of white sensibility, and a high dose of denial of the settler-racist-colonial past and the continued symptoms of white supremacy, suggest that silence is better than a clearly articulated question of land. It is in the political arrangement of the negotiated settlement that the land question should irritate white sensibilities. The Constitution, with its all-embracing notion of sameness, dilutes the fact that the conception of land is different for whites and for blacks. And there is a concerted effort in the erasure of being of the black to render the conception of race as something of no significance. The Constitution assumes that the land question will be resolved by introducing reforms like redistribution, restitution and tenure, which will never work in this racist-settler-colonial matrix. It has nothing to offer in terms of the land question, due to the absence in it of a conception of being and a direct confrontation with history. As things stand, the Constitution creates an impasse in so far as it is ahistorical and far removed from the existential realities of land dispossession and the ontological presence of blackness. There is a need to resolve the land question without divorcing it from the conception of being. The land question as defined in the framework of the Constitution does not regard the landless as subjects who are qualified to own land. The latter are the poor and the damned, who are made not subjects but objects, still caught in the history of violence, exclusion and dispossession. This means that a political intervention has guaranteed the victorious site to the status quo, as land ownership is still racially marked.

Solutions contained in the Constitution that are said to resolve the land question have not worked at all. In fact, they were not designed to work in the first place. For the land question has not been formulated in the interests of the black. Here is an unnecessary impasse: the African National Congress has been vacillating between, on the one hand, wanting land expropriation without compensation and, on the other, what is called 'just and equitable' compensation (Republic of South Africa 1996, Section 25.3). These are empty rhetorical positions as this is the party in power, and it refuses to use its power to change the Constitution. The land question, for the African National Congress, has been a matter of election sloganeering and not a policy issue. The Economic Freedom Fighters have made pronouncements on the land question, with a push for expropriation without compensation. But the contradiction in their positions has always been that they remain faithful to the Constitution and the Freedom Charter. In fact, both the African National Congress and the Economic Freedom Fighters maintain the same position, with differing cosmetic overtones: both political parties are not in favour of dismantling the Constitution, but argue for its 'amendment' by 'constitutional means'. Thus they are both hemmed in by its legality. It is the settler-colonial polity that is using the Constitution to the full extent of its might, and using the juridical muscle it has through the courts to do so (courts which are still settler-colonialist by virtue of being based on Roman-Dutch law, the legal spirit of South Africa, the judiciary not having been transformed notwithstanding the post-1994 dispensation). The courts have become the turf of victory that ensures settler-colonial land theft remains intact.

The historical land claims articulated and practised by Black First Land First, with its 'Land or Death' code, are constitutionally criminalized (Kunene 2019). Without irony, this criminalization comes from the Freedom Front Plus, Solidarity and AfriForum, which, with their Afrikaner and racist attachments disguised as concern for 'minority rights', have the sympathetic ear of the judiciary and the African National Congress, as the governing regime fears this Afrikanerdom polity. The settler-colonial land theft, when called out by Black First Land First, is regarded as unconstitutional. And absurdly, Black First

Land First has been burned for being unconstitutional as it is the only movement of the black. But there is nothing seen as unconstitutional in regard to the Freedom Front Plus, Solidarity and AfriForum, whose ideology is infused with Nazi and fascist ideological fibre. Just because they cry minority rights and claim to be constitutional, they are seen as legal, while the blacks' only formation is criminalized. The Constitution, in its liberal form, is fundamentally against the return of the stolen land.

It is apparent that the land question is forever eclipsed. That is why the instrumentalist vices of the property clause in the Constitution exist, in that they concern themselves with what is practical and what is not. The pragmatic imagination has not actualized anything to counter the continued plague of landlessness. It is imperative to go beyond Ntsebeza's (2005) constitutional critique qua reform and extend the critique to existential questions that unearth the ontological scandal. This is to centre the conception of being that the Constitution erases, an erasure which could even imply that blacks cannot own land.

The land question and social movements

The rupture of subjectivity of the landless through the formation of short-lived social movements heralded a watershed moment for the land question. This was to be the area of politics where the articulation of the political demands for land would come into being. This was interesting, but what remained unobserved was that these struggles were nothing but a white leftist agenda for controlling the suffering of blacks. Since the land question was not *stricto sensu* locked in the rural/urban binary, most people in the urban areas saw their plight being linked to their rural counterparts as they faced forced removals (Alexander 2004). Thus, the white left hijacked the struggle of blacks to make demands for land and turned it into pseudo-solidarity politics. What is also of interest is that the formation of social movements, and in particular those dealing with land, has had to do with the rural setting. But the engagements with the land question have been more a part of urban politics. There have not been strong national rural social movements that advocate for the land question; there have been some rural movements but they have made no national impact.

Social movements were assisted by non-governmental organizations in terms of advocacy, research, planning, mobilization and policy engagement. The role of land sector 'civil society' quickly shifted from supporting oppositional struggle to carrying out the technical work of information dissemination, capacity building, legal support, research, mediation and many other interventions and strategies. As Amanda Alexander (2004) shows, the interventions on land reform by the social movements were aimed at identifying and closing the legal and bureaucratic gaps in land reform programmes.

The rise of social movements like the Landless People's Movement, Abahlali baseMjondolo (the shack dwellers' movement) and the Anti-Eviction Campaign was a response to the disillusionment with the African National Congress project and the rise of the oppressed. The focus here will be on the Landless People's Movement, which emerged in 2001. Its famous campaign was entitled 'Landlessness = Racism', and this was given visibility in the United Nations World Conference Against Racism (Hall 2004a, 2004b). As Ntsebeza (2007) notes, the Landless People's Movement was formed in response to the frustration and discontent of the landless, and the events unfolding in Zimbabwe at the time played a key role. Added to this has been the Landless People's Movement's connection with the Brazilian Landless Workers' Movement and La Via Campesina (the international movement of peasants) as well as the Zapatista

Movement. Alexander (2004) correctly notes that the Landless People's Movement's focus is on advocating for change in the national land policy, but it also finds itself having to be on the defensive by preventing evictions from rural farms, urban settlements and apartment complexes.

The Landless People's Movement was founded on two grounds. Firstly, frustration with the failure of post-1994 South African land reform, which does not address the plight of the landless but defends the current landowners. Secondly, the African National Congress-led government's abandonment of the social democratic ideals that had shaped its Reconstruction and Development Programme (Republic of South Africa 1994) in favour of neo-liberal goals (as expressed in the Growth, Employment and Redistribution plan that replaced this programme [Department of Finance 1996]). The Landless People's Movement was small in terms of capacity, but it was able to draw attention to and provoke debate around the land question; however, despite its best efforts little was achieved in this regard. It was in 2004 that the Landless People's Movement engaged in a campaign, 'No Land! No Vote!', calling for the poor and the landless not to vote in the 2004 general elections (Alexander 2004). It accused South Africa of not having achieved genuine liberation, and this campaign was supported even by the Anti-Eviction Campaign based in the Western Cape.

The Landless People's Movement drew its support from those who were landless, and the ideal was to address the landlessness of both rural and urban (township and informal settlement) residents. Through its organizing practices and demands and in its political articulation, the Landless People's Movement showed how the rural and urban struggles of landlessness are linked far more than a politicized dichotomy will allow (Alexander 2004). The organization is based in

Johannesburg, and this means the leadership is urban but with rural connections. However, it is not a national body, meaning that it has not penetrated the national political scene by having branches all over the country.

According to Hall (2004b), the Landless People's Movement has made the rural constituency visible on the political scene. This, however, is in the manner of representation of it, and not in the rural community itself taking the lead on matters that affect it. Still, Hall acknowledges the fact that the Landless People's Movement has given voice to the voiceless and has bridged the gap between the urban and rural land struggles. What links these two geographical settings is the question of landlessness. What is railed against are the narratives which maintain that the land question should be urbanized, individualized and monetized to be of benefit to modernized forms of ownership. For the Landless People's Movement, of course, what was on the agenda was to address the land question and the fact that the land should return to its rightful owners. It located its political activism in relation to the historical context in which the return of the land would mean true liberation. The close working relationship between the Landless People's Movement and the civil society sector really helped it in pressing the land question. However, the unforeseen pitfalls it encountered, with the politics of liberation being hijacked and controlled by white leftists, are yet another scandal to be referred to.

Obviously, the Landless People's Movement is not as vibrant today as it was in its early years. This can be attributed to the factional politics and infighting that plagued the movement, and to its falling under the grip of the white left's tutelage. In entrenching themselves in supposed solidarity with the plight of the landless, the white left controlled the struggle of the Landless People's Movement. It is on these grounds that the

shift in the organization's agenda took place, and the agenda of
the left became the agenda of the Landless People's Movement,
something that remains unacknowledged. A significant instance
of this shift took place in Protea South in Soweto, where the
leadership was located. Maureen Mnisi was the leader of the
Landless People's Movement, and was outspoken as the face of
the movement. But it was the white leftists who increasingly
gave guidance on the demands the movement should make and
how this should be done, which showed that Mnisi, as the leader
of the movement, was not in charge of the revolution. Henrick
Böhmke (2010b, 11) writes: 'From the outset, all fledgling movements attracted a coterie of middle-class, left-leaning activists
and academics, some newcomers and some remnants of earlier
disaffections with the "revolution betrayed", searching for a new
radical social agent'. The politics of representation have clouded
social movements, in that those who are affected have their revolutionary plight both exacerbated and yet also assisted. The white
leftists are serving the same structure of subjection, in that they
articulate the demands of the landless for land knowing that this
is not to their benefit, in effect leading black organizations while
misleading them. They are speaking and acting on behalf of the
landless while being themselves the beneficiaries of the land.
Their acts, in no uncertain terms, are contributing to the very
subjection of landlessness, since they are engaged in what Linda
Alcoff (1991) refers to as the problem of speaking for others. The
white leftists are involved in an ontological struggle that is not
theirs, and this is not necessarily wrong, but it is entirely wrong
if they dictate the terms of this ontological struggle. White leftists adopted a tutelage role to help the landless through court
cases, workshops on capacity building, tactics of protest and the
register through which demands should be made. What comes
out in these acts of civil society generosity by the white leftists

is that the landless are not on their own, as they would like to present themselves to be, but are instead, to put it in the terms coined by Frantz Fanon (1967, 220), being 'acted upon'. The indictment uttered by Fanon (1967, 117) is that 'the future will have no pity for those men, possessing the exceptional privilege of being able to speak worlds of truth to their oppressors, [who] have taken refuge in an attitude of passivity, of mute indifference, and sometimes of cold complicity'. Fanon reminds the vanguard of the Landless People's Movement not to forget their existential quandary – that is, what is at stake in relation to their landlessness – as opposed to engaging in the struggle as fashioned by the white leftists. To see the latter as an important ally in their struggle for land is to miss the mark that the struggle is theirs – only theirs.

The point to be made is that the white leftists are not landless, and they also remain untouched by the violent history of land dispossession and its aftermath. Therefore, their involvement in the landless struggle through leftist tutelage is nothing but a scandal. According to Böhmke (2010a), the white leftists are engaged in the romanticization of the Landless People's Movement by taking the 'ethical baton' to make the ethical demands of the landless. This is to make the voice of the landless heard, not through the subjectivity of the landless, but rather through the ideological episteme of the white leftists. Even if it will be the black body speaking, its subjectivity is the exteriority, while the interiority of white leftist subjectivity, if linked to land, is just the mask of a fiat. The plight of the landless is the presence that is absent in terms of being, in that the conception of land is seen in its own right and disconnected from being. According to Böhmke (2010b, 22), the landless are duped by 'the hue of civil graces', that is, the solidarity gestures and political subjectivities managed by the white leftists as if they share the same plight. It is true that social movements have been commercialized through civil society politics by the white leftists, and it is also true that these social movements are nothing but research subjects. Within the leadership and its upper strata everything is just ceremonial in terms of power, and this amounts to the politics of fronting. The latter can also be said about the Landless People's Movement, which appears to be 'resolutely militant and possessed of unusual clarity and courage' (Böhmke 2010a), while at the same time being deputized by the white left.

Moreover, Böhmke (2010a) rightly points out that this leads to the 'creation of poetic myths', something which is beneficial to the branding of social movements and the Landless People's Movement in particular. The major preoccupation is the politics of protest, due process and the mask of judicial victory. This is nothing other than bourgeois preoccupation and has nothing to do with land as a fundamental question that needs historical accounting. The demands of the Landless People's Movement were radically altered from what they had originally been. The demands for land now became 'service delivery' demands – that is, demands for a matchbox house, a toilet, water and sanitation. However important, the latter demands have nothing to do with land in their ontological register. The demand for land is larger: it is the demand for land *in toto*. This alteration of demands was not accidental but deliberate on the part of the white leftists, in that they oversaw the strategies of the Landless People's Movement and the content of their register of demands. In the Landless People's Movement's subjectivity there is no centrality of being, or land as the embodiment of being.

The notion of the 'solidarity collective' is oxymoronic in that no mention is made of the ontological demands that put the historical question of racist-settler-colonial land theft at the centre. It is interesting that the Landless People's Movement's demands are not directed at this historical scandal, as they were in its formative years. The land question, when it comes to the Landless People's Movement, is tamed, and its basis of resistance is misdirected. Therefore, the Landless People's Movement is not what it was: at its inception it wanted to bring an end to landlessness, but this landlessness continues.

The persistence of the absence of being

If the absence of being persists in the land question, there is no way that this question will be resolved. The land question is not contemporary, and its historical specificity is the racist-settler-colonial triad. The land question must be confronted with this triad, and such a confrontation means that the ontological position – the existential conception of being affixed to land – will be affirmed in calling for the politics of reparations. This means that the form and content of the land question are not complete without being. It is necessary to challenge the post-1994 South African narratives that place emphasis on pragmatism and its articulations, which are devoid of political imagination and are caught in the instrumentalist subjectivity of policy formulation and punditry. This means that the more elite and urbanite subjectivities take the position of officialdom, and land reform is to be understood through their dictates. It is this elitist and urban legendary tale that is challenged, because it does not address and engage the land question robustly. According to Sam Moyo (2007), this tale simply privileges the advocacy of market-based methods of land reform, which are blocking genuine land reform and offer no alternatives. This position undermines efforts to break the racist-settler-colonial land monopoly. It is this subjectivity which puts more emphasis on land without being, and also downplays the triad of historical specificity.

Furthermore, the form of subjectivity that needs to be amplified is that which privileges the plight of the landless and their need to overcome the hellish existential conditions they are trapped in. For their existential condition is truth enough, without any qualification by policy makers and pundits. Their existential condition is that of precariousness, and as Mngxitama (2009) states, they are caught in the dispossession of land, dispossession of labour and dispossession of being. It is this triad of dispossessions that creates the ontological status of what Fanon (1969) terms 'wretchedness'. To amplify, Mabogo More (2011, 179) writes: 'Fanon similarly contends that the land remains the fundamental object of colonial-racial conflict and violence'. It is this historical plague that creates wretchedness, which entrenches itself in the form of landlessness.

In a politics of liberation that calls for new creation of being, the land question cannot be a mere footnote. The land which was stolen and remains in those hands is supposed to be restored through reparations. But the latter is an alarm call to the post-1994 discourse in the sense that this is seen as something akin to apocalypse; and Zimbabwe is made an example because it undertook a more robust land reform intervention. For sure, land reform in that country has been fraught with violence, but the other face of violence is the structural injustice whereby racist-settler-colonial subjects owned land whereas Zimbabweans were landless. It is clear that only one part of the narrative has been peddled in the silencing and name-calling directed against other narratives. In the Zimbabwean land discourse there has been a poverty of competing narratives, and only the story of the landowners was peddled at the expense of the landless. When the land question in post-1994 South Africa is raised, it is often remarked that this country will go the Zimbabwean route. This then implies that the racist-settler-colonial land theft is legitimate and should not be challenged.

It is important to imagine another political register through which the land question should be engaged; this would mean taking the subjectivities of the landless seriously by admitting the fact that the land question is nothing but a question of land theft and restoration. The land which was stolen should be restored through reparation in order to end the landlessness that still plagues the majority of black South Africans. It is clear that the land question cannot be a peripheral matter, or a matter to be postponed. It cannot be foreclosed, due to the fact that land qua being is the affixed entity. There cannot be liberation of being without land. It is this actualization that should bring to a halt the politics of possession and dispossession. As Ewa Ziarek (2001) argues, the possession of objects is the politics of the being as the object of control, and that ontological entity not being able to be in possession of its subjecthood. It is in this existential crisis that being is alienated from its land and itself. As Ziarek contends, there is a need to resignify the experience of dispossession, and this is where being will be the ethical schema through which the demands of liberation should be actualized.

Ultimately, the form and content of liberation are the desire and actualization of ending the *longue durée* triad of dispossession sketched earlier. The resignification of experience creates new subjectivities concerning the land question and articulations of the land question from the perspective of reparation, rather than protecting the present forms of ownership. 'Manifesting itself as an interruption of the originary identification, the ethical schema expels the I out of itself and exposes it to radical exteriority' (Ziarek 2001, 7). The conception of being is not the 'I', but the collective entity which was violated by racist-settler-colonial violence. It is this violence that created landlessness of being through rapacious forms of dehumanization. It is infused with sadistic impulses to realize the devastating effects of dehumanization. Therefore, this violence does not focus on the 'I' in the individual sense, but on a collective being of blackness. This is because land was not dispossessed from an individual but from a collective entity, which led to the psychic injury in the ontology of blackness. The current land reform programmes will continue to fail as they are preoccupied with the 'I', the very entity that is exterior to the conception of being in existential terms of land dispossession.

In the final analysis, it is important to state that the landless are not existing entities; through the acts of systematic and systemic dehumanization of racist-settler-colonial tyranny they are rendered functionally dead. Landlessness is dehumanization par excellence, and there cannot be any being and land if there is dehumanization. This therefore points correctly to the fact that the emergence of being as a subject is at the same time the articulation of the land. The struggle is ontological, and More (2011) captures it as the struggle for land and bread. This is the ontological horizon that the post-1994 South African neo-liberal state did not inaugurate, so it must be relentlessly pursued. For there to be an end to the ontological scandal, land cannot be articulated outside the ambit of being, and reparations should be the main item on the political agenda – it is here that liberation will be inaugurated. The politics of the necessity of being and land are embedded in this possibility.

The land question has been a long-standing item on the political agenda. It cannot be avoided with the excuse that it is a difficult and sensitive issue that will create a fault line in the nation, as if there are not already fault lines of possession and dispossession. The fault line has been institutionalized, normalized and naturalized through the banality of neo-liberal dogma with its dictum: 'there is no alternative'. This cannot be the order of things, as if there had been a historical accident. In point of fact, there was and there is a history of racist-settler-colonial land theft, and its infrastructure is a continuing reality – an ontological scandal. The land question is not a quandary; it is a soluble question that can be addressed through the politics of reparations. If this is not done, it means that the racist-settler-colonial legacy which haunts post-1994 South Africa through existential asymmetry and injustice is legitimate.

Being and land are inseparable, and this is where the subjectivity of the landless is rooted. Articulating their ontological demands must depend on the subjectivity of the landless themselves, and must not be acted upon by exterior agents. It is through being acted upon by these agents that the demands for land reparations will fail to be realized, as the original demands will be altered. There cannot be faith that the post-1994 South African neo-liberal reality will address the land question because it does not take it seriously, and is more concerned with the sensibilities of the past and with market forces. There cannot be faith in the Constitution, as it protects the racist-settler-colonial land theft. There cannot be faith in the white leftists, as their interests are not in reparations but in controlling the Landless People's Movement's struggle and turning its demands into concerns about service delivery. Where should faith be placed if not in the landless themselves? The struggle for land is yet to be realized, and it should be achieved by confronting the racist-settler-colonial land theft in accordance with being qua land. Thus, the land question will not be a floating signifier but the ontological specificity for rehumanization and liberation. The ownership of land should reside in the living community that is founded upon the land. The life that comes out of land ownership – as opposed to land dispossession, which is the absence of the ontological – is life qua life. It is a necessity that being and land are the sedimentation of the inseparable.

3 | Steve Biko: The Matter of Ante-Marx(ism)

There is a silent historical scandal whose record, archive and ledger book are marked by conquest.

What confronts Karl Marx and Marxism is the conquest of those who do not exist in the factory as workers, but who are in a world that dehumanizes them because they are racialized as black, and their humanity cannot be accounted for as it is perpetually questioned by the racist mechanics and machinations that underwrite conquest and its epochal intensification and elaboration. The scandal concerns those who are black-in-an-antiblack-world.

Conquest, as a matter of thought, is that problematic that continues to haunt the annals of Azanian existential tradition, which is rooted in manifest different, complex, expansive, parallel, interlocking, intersecting resistances that began with the colonial encounter and have continued right through its (un)folding(s) in various streams of antagonisms that still mark the contemporary. These antagonisms are also marked by what Marx(ism) disavows. Antiblackness, which underwrites the operating logics of Marx(ism), is what the Azanian existential tradition exposes, because conquest is the principal marker of this tradition, one that will never be erased by any form of fabrication, censure and *ad hominem* dismissal.

Marx(ism) does not account for the idea of conquest, and there is no reparatory inscription that can come through communism to remedy the pain and suffering inaugurated and perpetuated by the *longue durée* of this conquest. This was challenged, and is still challenged, by the Azanian existential tradition. This tradition gives primacy to the name Azania, as opposed to South Africa. It is a tradition that finds content and form in the philosophy of existence. Indeed, this tradition does not originate in or from Marx, nor does it find its content and expression in what came with, through, or after Marx – that is to say, Marxism (also a tradition of many registers, typologies, codes, canons, ideologies, philosophies, materialities, agendas, doctrines, strategies and inflections, depending on the context or events it is connected to, and generated by its originary inscription, which does not redress conquest since class is its fulcrum).

The Azanian existential tradition makes a call for reparations, and acts in the agitation of its articulation and actualization – that is, for a liberated Azania. But this is met with the dissimulation of conquest, and the idea of South Africa has been pushed to such an extent that even the colonial question is disentangled from conquest.

In the contemporary moment, the focus is on apartheid, as if there were no prior regimes of brutality of which apartheid became the heightened perfection. The Azanian existential tradition, in its ante-Marx(ism) stance and standing, is angular – it has a clear shape in terms of its sharp points of critique; thus, it annotates the historical record through fidelity to the memory of the long history of dispossession that began with the 1652 conquest. It is a radical refusal to erase violent inscriptions of conquest that founded and facilitated the dispossession of those who fought and continue to fight in the name of land, bread and humanity, rather than in the name of freedom, justice and equality – values propagated by a conquest that still reigns in dissimulated forms.

In this radical refusal to forget, the Azanian existential tradition, having given birth and rebirth to many existential struggles against conquest, has been fused with a philosophical intonation by Steve Biko, a founder of the Black Consciousness Movement, who was influenced by the Pan Africanist Congress led by Robert Sobukwe; and the name 'Black Consciousness' came to be the embodiment of what can be declared a philosophy of existence. Existence, here, should be taken seriously as the imperative to make life, even in conditions that are negating that life.

The concept of conquest accounts for the long history that demands critical diagnostics that are ante-Marx(ism). The critical analysis developed by Biko, having evolved from the political thinking of the Pan Africanist Congress – albeit in a radically different form – and from all Azanian existential traditions that predate it, finds expression in a mode of operation that cannot be referred to as dialectical, but rather as diagnostic, since it is engaged with a long history of dispossession. Infused with an unbreakable spirit, expressed in the call for Azania, the struggle for land, bread and humanity is not one of compromise.

The protocols that inform this call for Azania are declaring from the outset that in naming a territory, a radical distinction must be made between the names given to it by the conquerer and the conquered, and this naming involves the radical unfolding of the politics and the existential struggles that are executed in the name of these names. In the name of Azania, Biko saw it as key to continue the long black radical anticolonial struggle, and the problem he focused on in his elaboration of Black Consciousness philosophy's critical diagnostic was that conquest did not begin with the introduction of formal apartheid. In this philosophy, a philosophy of existence, liberation was the imperative.

Marx(ism) and conquest

A problem for Marx(ism)'s thought has been the figure of the black 'working things out' through a rigorous philosophical diagnostic that involves figuring, disfiguring and reconfiguring conquest. Marxism is structured outside the remit of this problematic. The question of conquest is the grammar of the existential struggle for Azania. And the principal inscription of this struggle, in this settler-colonial territory, is a demand for total liberation.

Racism is still, to this day, a marker of the racist-settler-colonial-segregationist-apartheid-liberal-constitutionalist apparatus, and it is a solid base that Marx(ism) disavows by deleting it from the historical record, archive and ledger book of the contemporary, dealing instead with race as merely symptomatic of other sites of antagonism, and thus irrelevant as a fundamental question.

The class that is seen as revolutionary by Karl Marx and Friedrich Engels (1968, 52), the one that is seen as the vanguard of the revolution, the only class, is the proletariat – the class whose 'rupture' with 'traditional ideas' effects revolutionary change in history. The antagonism is between the bourgeoisie and the proletariat – what Marx and Engels term 'class antagonism'. This antagonism goes through various stages; it unfolds in different historical epochs. As Marx and Engels (1968, 52) assert, 'the history of all past society has consisted in the development of class antagonisms that assume different forms [in] different epochs'. The reason for this antagonism is the 'exploitation of the many by the few' (Marx and Engels 1968, 47). So, the revolutionary call has been to create a push for capital to be in crisis, for it to end, for the very end of exploitation. Vladimir Lenin (1980, 8) writes: 'It was said that the "theory of collapse" to which capitalism is heading was unsound, owing to the tendency of class antagonisms to become milder and less acute'. But, writing with conviction, he stated that there would be a revolutionary triumph. According to Lenin (1962, 47), 'the proletariat will wage a broad and open struggle for the elimination of economic slavery, the true source of the religious humbugging of mankind'. This is exploitation, it is not conquest. It is all a matter of labour, not dehumanization on the grand scale where everything is structured by racism – the concept of exploitation cannot account for this.

As Herbert Vilakazi (1980) states, racism intensified with the intensification of capitalism. There is no decoupling of racism and capitalism. The logic of capital is structured by targeting the black body as the site of extraction, accumulation and disposal. It is under the logic of capitalism that racism is heightened and elaborated in ways that border on excess. This excess leads to the black becoming the thing that is used, misused and abused relentlessly. It is, in point of fact, the intensification of racism. And the ownership of capital is oligarchic. It is the few racialized whites who, in industrializing black labour, channel capital from the sweat, tears and blood of blacks to ensure that there is white privilege. According to Jacques Lezra (2018, 60), 'capital leaves its insular theoretical home and gets underway abroad, to be articulated with distinct political administrative forms (colonialism, imperialism)'. Frank Wilderson (2003a, 229) boldly states that 'capital was kickstarted by the rape of the African continent'. This phenomenon is, according to Wilderson, not principal in Marx(ism).

The long history of conquest, in its inaugural form, cannot be read outside race as a marker to justify the extractive logics of capitalism that are defended by law. As Anthony Farley (2008, 953) states, 'law begins as the masters come together as one, as Leviathan. Masters come together as mark'. This mark gives them the power to conquer, to name, to declare, to invent, to maim and so on. 'The inaugural dispossession is occasioned by the violence of the mark' (Farley 2008, 955).

> The mark shows who is to own and who is to be owned. The mark is the first and the last and enduring moment in the history of ownership because ownership of things is first and last the ownership of people. The flesh is marked and the would-be owners direct their violence of dispossession against those marked for violent dispossession (Middle Passage, Manifest Destiny, Infinite Justice and so on). (Farley 2008, 954)

The mark has been there as that which subjects the black through the technology of antiblack racism. Since the black is reduced to flesh, this is a way of turning the black into a thing, the non-sentient object to which all objectifications and abjections are directed. This creates the state in which the blacks are owned, and are not beings who are *their own*. In settler-colonialism, there is the figure of the white who is the owner. That is why those who own do so by means of conquest.

> Ownership means ownership by some and not by all. And ownership means that the entire world must come to be owned, otherwise there would be an exodus of the dispossessed from the spaces of their possession. Those who own are owners. Those who do not own are themselves owned. The non-owners are owned, like things, by the owners ... and the owned must surrender

themselves to the class or collective will of the owners or die. (Farley 2008, 954)

This is what conquest is. The owners who mark come together, in their will to own, as what Nelson Maldonado-Torres (2008a, 13) calls a 'community of masters' who are driven by 'genocidal impulses' to make ways for conquest to be unimpeded. The history of the mark is the one that the black radical tradition in general, and the Azanian existential tradition in particular, are rooted in. Cedric Robinson (2000, 184) testifies thus: 'There the struggle is more than words or ideas but life itself'. It is the history of a violent mark – white-over-black – and Farley (2008, 955) states that 'the injury is fatal'. This history, which injures from one epoch to the next, structured in the mark, is one that is ante-Marx(ism), or anti-Marx(ism); it is the mark that continues to dodge the fundamental question of conquest.

For Marx and Engels (1968, 35), there is no history but 'the history of class struggle'. Alex Callinicos puts this claim audaciously:

Marxism's theoretical foundations are radically different from those of any sort of nationalist ideology. For Marxism, the motor of history is the class struggle. It follows that the main conflict in modern society is that between the international working class and the international capitalist class. National divisions are secondary compared to the class struggle, and constitute simply a peculiar form taken by that struggle. (Callinicos 1989, 4)

There is in Marxism no history of conquest and resistance – the history of the black radical tradition, and more specifically for

Biko, the history of the Azanian existential tradition – only the history of the class struggle. As Mabogo More (2017, 230) notes: 'For the Marxists, for example, racism is a subspecies of class exploitation'. The history of conquest is disavowed. What Marx (1968b) terms 'world-historic struggle' does not account for the struggles against conquest. The struggle that is waged by the proletariat is not that of conquest in the colonies.

Marx (1968b) is concerned with the revolt of the proletariat against capital. As Marx (1968b, 115) states: 'The revolution thus moves along an ascending line'. This ascension, as Marx (1968b, 116) remarks, would see 'antagonisms that periodically seem to work themselves up to a climax only to lose their sharpness and fall away without being able to resolve themselves'. Focusing on Europe, he outlines this flux as a teleological unfolding, and this is not the reality in the colony. It is clear that Marx and Engels were addressing conditions in Europe, as evidenced by their famous line in the 'Manifesto of the Communist Party' which reads: 'A specter is haunting Europe – the specter of Communism' (Marx and Engels 1968, 35). It is a spectre that will haunt only Europe, and not the colonies. Even if the latter were to be haunted, this haunting spirit would still be the European one. But there is a spectre that is haunting the colonies – one that is absent from the grammar of Marx(ism). Roland Barthes (2015, 13) names it when he writes that 'racism isn't dead, it still has to be fought'. The spectre that Barthes points to is lurking in Europe, it is the thing that is the making of Europe itself. To raise matters that have to do with the spectre of race is to invite evasion, distortion, censure, ridicule and all the other tools of disavowal to say that race is not the issue, class is. The truth that Marxism cannot come to is the scandal raised by the black. 'And it was because the conditions of the black slave offend too flagrantly against the terms of that creed [of slavery] that the negro was really stripped of his quality as a human being and seen as a commodity' (Barthes 2015, 15).

Marx and Engels (1968) place emphasis on history, and it is logical for Biko to critique this position, as it is not his own history. And there is not even an attempt by Marxism in Azania to address the uncomfortable genealogy of conquest, where race is the marker. Even in the aftermath of conquest, in its spectral nature as something that still haunts, the critical diagnostics are ante-Marx(ist) in that the question of conquest, which still stands as the existential one, is not raised.

In the analytic of Marx(ism) there lies the silent scandal of colonial conquest. All that Marx and Engels (1968, 36) could say about this was: 'The discovery of America, the rounding of the Cape, opened up fresh ground for the rising bourgeoisie'. As to the extent to which this caused devastating effects of dispossession, they just mention this in passing, saying that this had been an unknown impulse of capitalism, and had led to development at a rapid pace that was unprecedented. Both Marx and Engels offer an examination that does not fit the questions that arise from the conquered. In point of fact, they persistently remain silent on the diabolical nature of this conquest, which Robinson (2000, 175) characterises as follows: 'The sum total was the dehumanization of Blacks'.

Clearly, conquest is the violent abstraction that Marx(ism) is not able to abstract. Nor is Marx(ism) capable of understanding black suffering. Class, as the marker, gets exhausted and becomes irrelevant when it comes to the ontological violation directed at the black body. 'This is to say violence towards black people is ontological and gratuitous as opposed to merely ideological and contingent' (Wilderson 2003a, 229). The Marxist conceptual arsenal – progress, alienation, exploitation, hegemony, civil society and the like – when it comes to the figure of the black creates what Wilderson (2003a, 229) calls a 'radical incoherence' and this is a scandal.

Biko and the Azanian existential tradition

The racism we meet does not only exist on an individual basis; it is also institutionalised to make it look like the South African way of life. Although of late there has been a feeble attempt to gloss over the overt racist elements of the system, it is still true that the system derives its nourishment from the existence of anti-black attitudes in society. (Biko 1978, 88)

Of the precise element of operationalizing racism, which is disavowed in Marx(ist) discourse, More (2008, 51) writes: 'Racism, therefore, is not discrimination alone, but also the power to control the lives of those excluded'. In a definition of the concept, Ramon Grosfoguel (2016, 10) notes that 'racism is a hierarchy of superiority/inferiority along the human line'. In conquest, the human line is marked clearly, and blacks are inferiorized below this line. This is done through the despotic exercise of power to ensure that subjugation and dehumanization are standardized and maintained. Biko asserts:

From this it is clear that as long as blacks are suffering from inferiority complex – a result of 300 years of deliberate oppression, denigration and derision – they will be useless as co-architects of a normal society where there is nothing else but man for his own sake. (Biko 1978, 21)

The dehumanization that comes through conquest, stripping bare the black's bodily being, has been the long history that continues with impunity. The beginning of it and its continuity have been intrusion that, for Jean-Luc Nancy (2002, 1), 'enters by force, through surprise or ruse, in any case without the right and without having first been admitted'. This intrusion is one that eliminates as it is not based on co-existence. It is the intrusion that lies at the heart of Marx(ism)'s scandal; even Marx(ism) does not refer to this intrusion by its violent name. Wilderson (2003b, 23) writes: 'A metaphor comes into being through violence that kills the thing such that the concept [of the thing] must live'. Since conquest is underwritten by logics of extraction, this has meant that white life is parasitic on black death. Even the logic of white privilege and black dispossession is based on this diabolical logic.

Robinson (2001, xxvii) formulates the concept of the 'just order'. He argues (2001, 105) that in its communal sensibilities, it stands antagonistic to 'greed', 'arrogance' and despotism. This ante-Marx(ist) disposition, which nonetheless finds its radical expression of Marxism in a radical critique of poverty and in its socialist ethos, led to the antagonism of classes. Those who are of this just order are, for Robinson, located in the polity that is laced with a fierce agency and outside the frame of Marx(ism). He deploys the concept 'un-Marxian mix' (2001, 120) to mark these ante-Marxist forces whose modes of inscription mark the 'agency of a radical philosophy'. This heretical site of inscription resonates very well with Black Consciousness not only as a radical philosophy, but as a philosophy of existence – Black Consciousness as a way of life, being-in-an-antiblack-world – and with a radical insistence on obliterating that world.

The demands of the black, as is clear in Biko's philosophical diagnostics, are deemed 'insatiable demands' by Wilderson (2003a, 231) as they cannot satisfy the rubrics of Marx(ism). What Marx and Engels (1968, 48) call 'Communistic abolition' remains mute when it comes to the doctrine of Discovery, and its rapacious unleashing of conquest. Where there is wage relation in terms of the worker, there is a non-waged relation to the slave. According to Wilderson (2003a, 230), the worker will demand that productivity be democratized and the slave will demand that productivity come to a halt, that it 'stop without recourse to its ultimate democratization'. This is the real structure of antagonism. The class antagonism happening within the Marxist framework cannot be imposed on those who are conquered, as they are not workers, but slaves.

This, according to Wilderson (2003b, 23), means that the 'slave has no symbolic currency or material labor power to exchange'. The reason for this is the absence of what Wilderson points to as the transaction of value. The slave and the worker are not the same. The worker, who is the subject of Marxism, is one confronted with 'symbolic rationality' as Wilderson (2003b, 23) states, and diametrically opposed is the conquered black being and slave who is confronted with 'despotic irrationality'.

The Azanian existential tradition is where Biko is located; thinking on this ante-Marx(ist) ground, he is concerned with the existential battlefield of ideas and concrete material facticities that animate the Azanian existential tradition's cartographies of struggle. As a philosopher of existence, one who is concerned with bread, land and humanity, Biko had to fully inscribe the philosophy of the *here* – that is, one rooted in the Azanian lived experience and the fact of blackness. Here is a famous dictum: 'The philosophers have only *interpreted* the world, in various ways; the point, however, is to *change* it' (Marx 1968a, 30, emphasis in the original). Surely, it is Marx who made this powerful conclusive mark. But here in the settler-colony, a philosopher did both. Who can it be if not Biko, speaking within the long Azanian existential tradition and the whole history of insurgent black struggles that surrounded his milieu of Black Consciousness? The emphasis of Marx's (1968a, 29) thought, which led to his dictum, is on that which should 'be criticized in theory and revolutionised in practice'. Marx makes a striking remark:

> However, we are not concerned here with the conditions of the colonies. The only thing that interests us is the secret discovered in the New World by the political economy of the Old World, and loudly proclaimed by it: that the capitalist mode of production and accumulation, and therefore capitalist private property as well, have for their fundamental condition the annihilation of that private property which rests on the labour of the individual himself . . . the expropriation of the worker. (Marx 1976, 94)

There, Marx makes it clear where his interest lies. Even though he states that slavery is what he calls the method and practice of 'primitive accumulation', the racialized and dehumanizing nature of this deadly logic is embalmed by brushing reality aside. Reiland Rabaka (2010, 148) rightfully states that 'racism and colonialism, always and everywhere, seem secondary in Marx's (and Marxists') works'.

Here is the picture of society that Marx and Engels (1968, 48) present: 'In bourgeois society, living labour is but a means to increase accumulated labour. In Communist society, accumulated labour is but a means to widen, to enrich, to promote the existence of the labourer'. This is alluring, but it is not fitting to the existential condition that Biko confronts in his existential struggle.

Marx and Engels (1968, 53) are correct when they write that 'political power, properly so called, is merely the organised power of the one class for oppressing another'. However, this oppression is, according to Marx, based on capital. He states that 'the wealth of the nation is once again, by its very nature, identical with the misery of the people' (Marx 1976, 938). Evidently, Marx made this observation in theorizing the colony. But still, the root of all this is capital. For in the destruction of the colony, according to Marx, capital is the problem. Marx (1976, 938) goes further to coin the term 'systematic colonization', but for him the logics of racialization are not there; capital is 'the root of the evil' as it is tied to property, and it is the destruction of this capital that 'would destroy . . . the colony'.

Biko, in his philosophy qua practice, engaged in the existential milieu he lived in, and his world is one that Marx disavowed. Biko's thought had to be grounded in facticity as a matter of necessity. In his reality, black bodies have been structurally and infrastructurally positioned to be at the receiving end of settler-colonialism's firepower and to legitimize its conquests. It is known that Marxism is impervious to this, hence the silent scandal about the name Azania itself. Marxism has no grammar to articulate the grand scale of dehumanization of blacks. Its principal limitation has been the valorization of class and disavowal of race. To challenge this limitation in Marx(ism), Biko drew from Frantz Fanon (1967), who focused on the lived experience of being-black-in-an-antiblack-world. In his ante- qua anti-Marxist position, Robinson (2000) correctly argues that the total configuration of the lived experience, the lived reality that is the human experience, demands other forms of engagement. This, according to Robinson, demands categorical expansion. Thus, the concretization and contextualization of what is at stake is principal. This is what Biko did, going even further to the extent of reconfiguration, where his philosophical diagnostics unmasked the long history of conquest and its continuities in the contemporary moment. Biko (1978) states that black people are expected not to act. They should take it all in, they must be passive and just suck it up. This is what he says about whites:

> This to me follows logically after their initial assumption that they, being a settler minority, can have the right to be supreme masters. If they could be cruel enough to cow the natives down with brutal force and install themselves as perpetual rulers in a foreign land, then anything else they do to the same black people becomes logical in terms of the initial cruelty. To expect justice from them is to be naïve. (Biko 1978, 74)

The philosophical diagnostics which Marx refuses to conduct are the ones that test the diabolical extent of the racist mechanics and machinations that institutionalize, naturalize and normalize dehumanization of the blacks. This, on the grand scale, has meant the marking of the black along the racial line, and the racist episteme prevailing to authorize and hierarchize who belongs and who does not in the settler-territory called South Africa. This territory has been lubricated by systematic, systemic and long-lasting dispossession of land, bread and humanity at different ontological sites (where those who are on-site are regarded as humans, and those who are off-site are regarded as slaves) – the destructions that are so grand that they overflow the historical record, archive and ledger book. And, in the ledger book, when it comes to accounting for the destruction that blacks have been at the receiving end of, even down to the contemporary moment, still there will be dissimulations of conquest. Therefore, the encounter and aftermath of this problematic should be thought as something ungraspable in Marx(ism)'s hands, owing to the fact that capital, in its racist mechanics and machinations, has been the extraction of the black flesh whose suspension as a sentient being has not been a problem that preoccupies Marxism in the settler-territory called the idea of South Africa. Biko's disposition has been embodied in the insistent call for decolonization – that is, for the reparability of dispossession, whose grammar of land, bread and humanity has been expressed in the name of Azania – which is the discursive absence in Marx(ism).

The name Azania is what is inaugural in actualizing the reparatory inscription of rewriting the whole field of the long history and its aftermath. This radical demand is not one that finds articulation and expression in Marx(ism). The understanding of the protocols of this reparatory inscription has been that the name South Africa is the authorization of the apparatus of dehumanization. In a radical way, Biko's disposition has been a thorough unveiling of what might blind.

Ante-Marx(ism), Biko goes to the Hegelian dialectic, and rigorously reconfigures it to really point out the matters at stake. In his philosophical diagnostics, he argues (1978, 51) that 'the overall analysis therefore, based on the Hegelian theory of dialectic materialism, is as follows. That since the thesis is a racism there can only be one valid antithesis i.e. a solid black unity to counterbalance the scale'. The originality of this diagnostic, being ante-Marx(ism) and going directly to Hegel and straight back to Azania in the spirit of facticity – that is, Biko's reconfiguration of the whole dialectic – is an argument for why blacks need to liberate themselves on their own and on their own terms. In solid affirmation of this, More (2008, 57) avers that 'the synthetic moment is a product of and therefore must be a higher expression of both the thetical and antithetical'.

First and foremost, this thinking will bring a clear under-standing of the existential problems to be confronted, and this means blacks doing it their own way, *by-themselves* and *as-themselves*. Biko (1978, 51) warns: 'One must immediately dispel the thought that Black Consciousness is merely a method-ology or means towards an end'.

> We do not need to apologise for this because it is true that the white systems have produced through the world a number of people who are not aware that they too are people. Our adherence to the values that we set for ourselves can also not be reversed because it will always be a lie to accept white values as necessarily the best. (Biko 1978, 51)

In its form and definition, Black Consciousness is ante-Marx(ism). Kogila Moodley (1991, 144) affirms this: 'Thus Black Consciousness emanated from the differential material and political circumstances in which blacks were situated'. More also amplifies Black Consciousness thus:

> The consciousness of a black person is an awareness of one's personhood as significantly different from the bodily appearance of other persons not designated black . . . In a racially white supremacist world, the consciousness of a person designated black invariably becomes a consciousness of a being whose humanity is perpetually at issue – or stated differently, a black person in such a world is a being such that because of its very blackness, [it] is always in question. (More 2017, 42)

It should be noted that in Marxism, too, the humanity of blacks is still questioned. Rabaka eloquently states:

> White workers, indeed, do profit from white supremacist colonialism, although their fiendish financial gains are more or less miniscule compared to those of the bourgeoisie and, furthermore, what is often overlooked is that a large part of what white workers reap is not monetary or material but . . . white supremacist *psychological support, and supplies*; white supremacist *injustice justifications and jurisdiction*; white supremacist *racial resources and reserves*; and, white supremacist *cultural capital and claims to human divinity and human dignity.* (Rabaka 2010, 154, emphasis in the original)

White supremacy is the base, and by disavowing that, Marxism is not even able to engage in 'antagonisms toward unwaged slavery, despotism, and/or terror' (Wilderson 2003a, 225). In fact, in conquest, it is not whites who are the conquered. It is whites conquering blacks, and the Marxist frame with its fabrication will not withstand the heat of this critical disposition that Biko, and the whole ensemble of black radical thinkers, have been turning on. Whiteness, as the social formation of Marxism, which then caused blacks who propagated it to structurally adjust their demands away from race as the structure of antagonism to class as the structure of antagonism, has meant the omission of the colonial crimes from the roll. In conquest, the black–white non-relation that Marxism does not want to confront has a scandal within it, namely that white Marxists, with their black Marxist deputies, will leave the infrastructure of conquest intact. This is whiteness in its reified and refined mode. 'Whiteness, then, and by extension civil society, cannot be solely "represented" as some monumentalized coherence of phallic signifiers, but must first be understood as a social formation of contemporaries who do not magnetize bullets' (Wilderson 2003b, 20). In conquest, whiteness has the firepower. So, those who are magnetically attracted to bullets are those marked black. The magnitude of the violence of conquest should be registered firmly. The black body was approached by capital with what Wilderson (2003b, 22) calls 'direct relations of force', not in the manner of 'approaching a white body with variable capital'.

Thus, Black Consciousness philosophy is a thought that is before Marx(ism). It is a thought that is even outside the grounding of Marx's body-and-geo politics, as Walter Mignolo (2011) puts it, in having to foreground the principality of the 'locus of enunciation' (Mignolo 2011, xv), where thinking where one is is the inscriptive force not only of rewriting being, but also of (re)politicizing that being to take the lived experience and the fact of being black seriously. This is what Biko's thought is, in the annals of Black Consciousness philosophy.

Black Consciousness against bad faith

White racism is what Marx(ism) in South Africa will disavow. Tired tropes like 'colonialism of a special type' will be abstracted in order not to deal with the elephant in the room – White Racism. Lou Turner gives this illuminating description:

> Historically, black resistance, rebellion, and revolution confronted the racialized violence of South African society as the very force of reason that white South Africa's masquerade of ethnoracial pluralism mono-polized as its moral ideal, but that it was woefully incapable of making real. It is according to this dialectic

that reason, resistance, and revolution form the historical material life of the black South African mind. (Turner 2008, 75)

As Turner (2008, 80) affirms, 'this, of course, is what Biko comprehends of the dialectic of racial domination in apartheid South Africa'. This is the very same dialectic, in its ante- and anti-Marx(ist) form, that will begin to mark Biko's profound originality. The synthetic thought of Biko, being reconfigurative of power, is in all matters original. It is an originality that stands against all forces that deny the facticity of what has been the issue at stake – white racism.

Black Consciousness has been against dissimulation, which is the spirit of 'bad faith', defined by Jean-Paul Sartre (1957, 65) as intentionally lying to oneself, and its recourse is the unconscious. Bad faith, according to Lewis Gordon (1995), is disavowing the truth of freedom and valorizing the pleasing falsehood that is antithetical to that freedom. According to Sartre, bad faith is not what one is. 'The goal of bad faith', says Sartre (1957, 65), 'is to put oneself out of reach; it is an escape'. Therefore, the act of denying oneself freedom to see things as they are, to see racism when it is dissimulated with the argument that it is class, constitutes bad faith. 'In this sense it is necessary that we *make ourselves* what we are' (Sartre 1957, 59, emphasis in the original). Echoing Sartre, Biko (1978, 49) rightfully exclaims: 'We want to attain the envisioned self which is a free self'. It is the self that is not in service of bad faith.

Black Consciousness, then, as the ante-Marx(ist) disposition, is a philosophy of being, the being of the black in the world that denies the humanity of the black. It is a philosophy that, according to More (2012, 24), is infused not only with struggle, 'but also [with] the politics of "being", that is, the politics of Black being in an antiblack world'. This is the being in service of good faith and not bad faith. This is the existentialist self – that is, 'Being-attuned' as per the formulation of Martin Heidegger (1962, 176) – where 'the world is constituted existentially by the state of mind'. It is from this state of mind that Black Consciousness will frame its politics of being by way of reconfiguration – that is, turning to the body as the site of questions.

Aimé Césaire (1972, 32) asks this question: 'What, fundamentally, is colonization?' Césaire's question remains unasked in Marx(ism). It presents a scandal in the ways that those who are in the condition of being-black-in-an-antiblack-world will pose it. For it is asked as a fundamental question and as such, each answer will be subjected to modes of questioning. This practice of questioning, this radical consistency, is clear in Fanon by way of a prayer:

> My final prayer:
> O my body, make of me always a man who questions!
> (Fanon 1967, 232)

It is this prayer that addresses the body whose humanity is questioned in order to legitimize conquest, a body that is racially marked, the body of the being in question. By turning to that body as a site of questions, a gesture which is unthinkable in Marx(ism), let alone in prayer, Fanon marks a completely different trajectory of what is at stake. Fanon's prayer is anchored by Mogobe Ramose (2007, 310): 'And thus we pray: "In the name of the peoples, against the conqueror and lost sovereignty. Amen"'. The Fanonian and Ramosean prayers are an indictment. These are not prayers that are asking for deliverance or whatever form of repentance. These prayers are charged with the spirit of revolt. These are the Azanian existential prayers. They are reparative in nature. The dispossession of land, bread and humanity is what is being fought against; this is the spirit that fuels these prayers, and symbiotically, these prayers also fuel that spirit. For these are prayers against the injustice, dehumanization and death that are thought, brought and wrought by conquest. The Fanonian and Ramosean prayers are, in the Azanian existential frame, ante-Marx(ism). They are foundational prayers, as they mark conquest as the source. These are prayers that, according to Huey Copeland (2016, 144), have not been 'rushing to the new' but have, in this spirited inscription whose eruptive and interruptive form, content, expression and practice, 'tended towards blackness – in all of its sensuous and imperceptible unfolding – that phantom site whose traces everywhere mark the construction of the material world and provide a different horizon from which to take our bearings'. These prayers are engaged in the radical refusal to forget. They are prayers against amnesia by way of reinscription of re-memoriality in the historical record, archive and ledger book. The Fanonian and Ramosean prayers are the quest for the end of dissimulation, as they insist on what Biko (1978, 98) affirms as 'a more human face'. They are prayers that make a more human face come face-to-face with a face behind layers of masks. These are prayers of blacks, and as Biko (1978, 59) says, they 'must have something to say about their oppression'. Indeed, this is what the Fanonian and Ramosean prayers are, as they say everything against oppression and everything for liberation.

The body is not the locus of enunciation in Marx(ism). Exploitation, alienation, surplus value, commodity value and so on do not have the somatic inflection that runs from Fanon through to Biko as its principal mark. Race is embodied. Class is purely disembodied. Blacks are overdetermined from without, as Fanon (1967) puts it, and this is at the level of the body that is marked below the human line because conquest has meant the annihilation of the black bodily being. According to the doctrine of Discovery, as Ramose (2018) shows, the black is nothing in the field of being, and should be conquered. Any violation of the black is right and just. It amounts to no kind of criminal act. To see the black is not to see a bodily being. Conquest, with its attendant force, led Césaire (1972, 42) to formulate the equation 'colonization = thingification'. This is further attested by Fanon (1967, 109) in his utterance of how the black is seen: '"Dirty nigger!" . . . "Look, a Negro"'. The dissolution of personhood, not as the result of exploitation but in what Robinson (2000, 171) marks as 'ontological totality', really shows the aptness of Biko's protocols of understanding the ontological questions of being-black-in-an-antiblack-world in relation to the doctrine of Discovery and the forces that it continues to unleash. Ontological totality, according to Robinson, is what should be preserved, and this is the matter of being. The continuing emphasis of Black Consciousness is on this preservatory force. It is here that there is no class as the marker; the fact and the lived experience of being black are the markers of colonization. In following Césaire, Fanon (1965, 126) affirms that 'the colonial situation standardizes relations, for it dichotomizes the colonial society in a marked way'.

Black Consciousness operationalized in politics

The dialectical reconfiguration undertaken by Biko, located in the concrete base of the black lived experience, gave impetus to politics. 'His genius included rendering politics *black*' (Gordon 2008, 88, emphasis in the original). Emphasizing the nature of politics, Biko (1978, 51) writes: 'However what we are concerned here with is group attitudes and group politics'. By politics, following Gordon (2008, 87), is meant a 'discursive opposition' against 'discursive enclosure'. This discursive enclosure means the closure of politics.

And for Black Consciousness, the operational definition of a way of life came to mean politics. Politics are a form of discursive opposition and Biko (1978, 65) attests that 'the essence of politics is to direct oneself to the group which holds power'. To say politics is to say Black Consciousness. The oppression Biko faced was, according to Gordon (2008, 88), 'a war on politics'. Black Consciousness is that discursive opposition that is in defence of politics. To be in defence of politics is to have what Adam Rosen-Carole (2015, 12) terms 'the right to unlimited critique', that possibility of creating a discursive condition of 'the mutual requirement of mutual authorization'. As Barnor Hesse (2011, 974) states, politics are a 'discursive form' that must be disentangled from racist inscriptions where whites are the only interlocutors and assume the policing function. For Hesse, politics are a site of antagonism, and they begin when there is discursive opposition. This form of antagonism stands in opposition to what Hesse (2011, 974) calls 'antagonistic policing'. The continued form of this policing creates a condition where, as Gordon (2008) states, war is declared on politics. When war is declared on politics, Black Consciousness will defend politics. Gordon (2008, 91) writes: 'If politics itself is what is at stake in the failure to address blackness, then there is no ironic conclusion that the contemporary South African state is also an antiblack one'. This is the conflict within politics themselves, and in Biko's case, these politics mean philosophically diagnosing power and that comes through the continued repoliticization of blackness.

> Black Consciousness is thus identical with political life, and those who are willing to take on the risk of politics in a context where a state has waged war against politics are, as opposition mounts, blackened by such a process. As a political concept, this makes the potential range of

Black Consciousness wide open to mean the collapse of
the antidemocratic state. (Gordon 2008, 89)

The insistence on a different set of conditions is what Black
Consciousness stands for, and this is the change brought about
by blacks themselves. This is the change brought about through
politics as a discursive opposition. Also, as a philosophy qua politics that is infused as life, a way of life, and a way of dwelling in
the lived experience of being-black-in-an-antiblack-world, Black
Consciousness philosophy has a clear stance regarding where it
is in the world: it is rooted in day-to-day life.

Standing against Marxism, the position of Black Consciousness has been that it takes the same stand in regard to white
liberalism. Black Consciousness, according to Moodley (1991,
146), 'represented the rejection of Marxism as white ideology
and its association with the South African Communist Party'.
This rejection is attuned to the fact that it is important for blacks
to think from their own existential condition. Thus, the quest
for definition is one principal mark. This definition would be
interdicted and policed in the Marxist discourse, whose contradictions do not deal with the existential condition that is structured by conquest. This mark, which Biko's operationalization of
Black Consciousness marks further by making a statement and
delivering a testament, has to do with the question of dissimulation. What is it that is being hidden?

What is hidden is white racism, the constitutive element of
conquest. White racism, Biko (1978, 23) affirms, 'rests squarely
on the laps of white society'. Therefore, this is the matter that
should be confronted by Marxism, instead of distracting blacks in
order not to name things for what they are. 'Thus in the ultimate
analysis no white person can escape being part of the oppressor
camp' (Biko 1978, 23). This is the fact that Biko brings to the fore

in concrete terms, and it has nothing to do with some philosophical abstractions. Even still, the extent of race denialism is the subterfuge whose subtextual inscription underwrites Marxism; it remains banal to the end as it still maintains that race is just an epiphenomenon. This line is tirelessly pulled out to gag black suffering. Blacks are even made to doubt that they themselves have conducted their philosophical diagnostics. Biko (1978, 23) retorts: 'Their presence amongst us is irksome and of a nuisance value'. As he exclaims (1978, 23), 'the blacks have heard enough of this'.

The problem of Marxism in the colonial situation

One trick that is used by Marxists in the colonial situation is to instil fear, and brand all the initiatives of blacks as lacking a 'good analysis' of the situation. With that didactic attitude, blacks are not allowed to think for themselves. It is in this Marxist didacticism that the racist superiory–inferiority relation of using class to mask racism, and to be silent on conquest, is formed, is made an orthodoxy, and blacks are not meant to veer off this script.

Marx and Engels (1968, 63) write: 'In short, the Communists everywhere support every revolutionary movement against the existing social and political order of things'. But seldom does this present itself as support; it is, rather, didacticism. Biko would have been receptive if blacks were supported by Marxists, but this turned out not to be the case. Didacticism has been one of Marxism's addictions. The irony is that Marx and Engels (1968, 50) argue that communism seeks to 'alter the character of that intervention, and to rescue education from the influence of the ruling class'. But there lies didacticism.

> The Communists, therefore, are on the one hand, practically, the most advanced and resolute section of the whole working-class parties of every country, that

section which pushes forward all others; on the other hand, theoretically, they have over the great mass of the proletariat the advantage of clearly understanding the line of march, the conditions, and the ultimate general results of the proletariat movement. (Marx and Engels 1968, 46)

Lenin (1992, 25) affirms that 'the culmination of this role is the proletarian dictatorship, the political rule of the proletariat'. Here is an evangelist posture in damnation and redemption just like the civilizational rhetoric.

The 'dangerous class', the social scum, that passively rotting mass thrown off by the lowest layers of old society, may, here and there, be swept into the movement by a proletarian revolution; its conditions of life, however prepare it far more for the part of a bribed fool of reactionary intrigue. (Marx and Engels 1968, 44)

What is interesting here is that both Marx and Engels are class-ists in the pejorative sense of the term. That is to say, they are discriminatory and their dehumanizing language is a testi-mony to this. There is not enough said about this dehumanizing language. The valorization of the working class will see even the whole Marxist framework being anti-peasant. This discrimi-nation is largely based on the issue of the working class being enlightened. In confirmation of this, Lenin (1962, 9) writes: 'Marx's philosophy is a consummate philosophical materialism which has provided mankind, and especially the working class, with powerful instruments of knowledge'. Marx and Engels were referring to their own Europeans. What more were those in the colonies – those that Fanon (1969) would call the wretched of the earth? It is not far-fetched to say they would, as a matter of their racialization, be an ultimate target of Marx's and Engels's salvo in its bloated racist intonations.

Ayi Kwei Armah (1984, 41) charges that 'Marxism, in its approach to the non-Western majority of the world's peoples, is demonstratively racist – racist in a prejudiced, determined, dishonest and unintelligent fashion'. Marx and Engels are steeped in civilizational logics that are not different from the conquerors that were there to civilize. The proletariat is, according to Marx and Engels (1968, 44), spirited 'with fresh elements of enlightenment and progress'. Armah (1984, 56) retorts: 'The dogma of proletarian rationality and suitability as revolutionary troops pervades Marxist literature'. And Roland Barthes comments as follows on the 'power of intimidation' of left-wing literature:

> Left-wing literature has, therefore, a power that is prior or external . . . Whatever its reality, it is a salutary myth, insofar as it helps to bring people together, draws the battle lines, unifies the forces and gives a name to the struggle. But there comes a point, all the same, when this reassuring expression has to be given an in-depth, rather than a broad, definition – when we have to go beyond its power of intimidation to its power of definition. (Barthes 2015, 29)

The didacticism of Marxism stems from the authoritative power it assumes. Those who advocate and propagate Marxism, and the proletariat as the premier class, are, in the words of Barthes (2015, 29), 'defined and united by the opinions they profess, the slogans they defend, the manifestos they sign, the congresses they attend and the magazines in which they write'. The broad framework of Marxist discursive modulations cannot account for the question of conquest. As Wilderson (2003a, 225) states, 'racism is read off the base, as it were, as being derivative of political economy'. But the rubrics of political economy do not account for the racism. And in the colony, the paradigm of political economy is not based on the reality of conquest and the racist infrastructures that it continues to consolidate.

What cannot be underestimated is the allure of Marxism. Robinson illuminates this thus:

> Marxism's intellectual power and pedigree, its promise of a hidden truth, its open opposition to insidious social order, its alternative mapping of the historical origins of the ruling classes, which they came to despise, and its identification with the underclass made it an almost irresistible companion. (Robinson 2000, 287–288)

Since Marxism is a philosophy of contradictions, its intellectual acumen, its rigour and spirited debate, its propensity for 'analysis', gave it great relevance for those who wanted to understand the existential condition. But, being hidden under the subject called the 'proletariat', or simply the worker, when it comes to the Azanian ground that is plagued by antiblack racism, as a mode of universal application the subject is found wanting. Armah gives a damning account of it:

> Marxism, in its approach to non-Western societies and values, is decidedly colonialist, Western, Eurocentric and hegemonist. Marxists do not present their philosophy as a Western variant of communist theory . . . Marxists in Africa exhibit a desire to institutionalize Western communist hypotheses as the only correct philosophy. Some of the most enthusiastic believers go

as far as to pretend to think that Marxism is not just a philosophy but a science, the only correct science of liberation. (Armah 1984, 41)

What Armah highlights is the Marxism of the South African Communist Party, a party which, even in the contemporary period, has no grammar to articulate conquest. But of course, this does not mean that Marxism is reducible to the South African Communist Party's version of it only, as there are many traditions of Marxism that have found expression in South Africa.

With its didactic character, Marxism becomes evangelical. And Biko, in opposition, writes:

I am against the intellectual arrogance of white people that makes them believe that white leadership is a *sine qua non* in this country and that whites are the divinely appointed pace-setters in progress. I am against the fact that a settler minority should impose an entire system of values on an indigenous group. (Biko 1978, 24)

This didacticism is problematic and Biko (1978, 24) says the following about it: 'It removes the focus of attention from essentials and shifts it to ill-defined philosophical concepts that are both irrelevant to the black man [sic] and merely a red herring across the track'. This has been a historical trick that continues to be repeated, and Marxists have been using it to warn blacks to be aware of 'contradictions'. But seldom is racism pointed out as the problem. Biko boldly declares the ill-defined nature of Marxism because it does not take as its point of departure the Fanonian fact of blackness and the lived experience of the black. Yet, audaciously, Marxism still wants to insist on its didacticism. By going it alone, and doing away with integrationist sensibilities,

Biko argues, blacks have to 'evolve a philosophy based on, and directed by, blacks' (1978, 67). Granted, Marxism is sound and rigorous. However, it is found wanting on the Césairean fundamental question, which is the base of a philosophy grounded and directed by blacks.

> Most white dissent groups are aware of the power wielded by the white power structure. They are quick to quote statistics on how big the defence budget is. They know how effectively the police and the army can control protesting black hordes – peaceful or otherwise. They know to what degree the black world is infiltrated by the security police. Hence they are completely convinced of the impotence of black people. (Biko 1978, 65)

A chief reason for this is to instil the culture of fear. Heidegger (1962, 179) places three marks on fear thus: 'That in the face of which we fear', 'fearing' and 'that about which we fear'. He elaborates on these marks (1962, 181) as follows: 'Whether privately or positively, fearing about something, as being-afraid in the face of something, always discloses equiprimordially entities within-the-world and Being-in – the former as threatening and the latter as threatened. Fear is a mode of state-of-mind'. Biko (1978, 78) gives this another dimension: 'The tripartite system of fear – that of whites fearing blacks, blacks fearing whites and the government fearing blacks and wishing to allay the fear amongst whites – makes it difficult to establish rapport amongst the two segments of the community'.

Black Consciousness against fear

Fear can be linked to bad faith in the form of the fear of freedom. It is this fear that will lead to petrification, and thus being immobilized, unable to act in the good faith of one's freedom. Indeed, conquest is terror, it arouses fear, and this fear is driven and imprinted in the whole bodily sensorium. Biko saw a possibility in his existential diagnostics, and gave an elaborate account of fear as a form of bad faith.

Conquest imprinted fear on the consciousness of the black, and pushed everything further into the realm of the unconscious, the interiority of the black, to cause destruction within and find a wrong outlet as the reaction to fear, directing the fear of whiteness towards the black by way of misdirected violence. Biko drew from the Azanian existential tradition of his ancestors, who did not fear but fought conquest even in the face of subjugation. Since fear, existentially, is essentially a state of mind, as Heidegger notes, Biko understood the importance of facing oneself in good faith so that fear can be faced, and he called for the purging and absolute expulsion of the fear that conquest imprinted on the minds of blacks.

Biko would come to embody the culture of fearlessness and would insist on the quest for freedom. According to Lindy Wilson (1991), Biko embraced the culture of fearlessness because Black Consciousness is a way of life, and he exhibited fearlessness in the face of the climate of fear.

> Black Consciousness took root and grew in spite of the awesome restrictions of the 1970s, when each year claimed more banned, and more detentions were made, often under the ferocious Section 6 of the Terrorism Act. With no access to lawyers, no certainty of being charged, detainees were often kept for months in solitary confinement, taken away from their work for a long period of time. (Wilson 1991, 50)

The Terrorism Act (No. 83 of 1967) was the weapon of apartheid. And as a weapon, it imprinted fear. Biko (1978, 74) highlighted the viciousness of this Act, together with the Suppression of Communism Act (No. 44 of 1950) and the Gatherings and Demonstrations Act (No. 52 of 1973): 'The strangest thing is that people are hauled in for most nothing to be tried under the most vicious of Acts – like the Terrorism Act'. Having to live under such dehumanization meant that fear was a marker.

> In human terms, to live under the threat of non-being is to live in what existentialists call a condition of finitude, the constant possibility of disintegration and death and, therefore, anguish and anxiety. The fundamental source of such anguish is the ever-present possibility of death. Apartheid racism is misanthropy, total and complete hate. It is the hated being of the Black victim. The original project of this hate is the total suppression of the Other's consciousness . . . (More 2012, 31)

This means having to face what Julia Suárez-Krabbe (2016, 3) refers to as the 'death project'. By showing the resolute desire to be free in these existentially obliterating conditions, the vanguard of Black Consciousness was placing itself in a precarious situation. As Leslie Hadfield (2016, 39) puts it, 'they also ran up against the "hostile wall" of a repressive state'. But no fear could reign.

In this climate of fear, the politics of being becomes the affirmative register of Black Consciousness, and the demand for liberation, to be achieved by any means, is clearly and forcefully pronounced and agitated for. The stakes are high and there is nothing to fear. For, indeed, what needs to be feared is fear itself. The very act of being terrorized should not leave the black terrified and trembling. No matter the cost of having to withstand the raw power of the oppressor, its firepower and all the modes of destruction that come with dehumanization, the black in Black Consciousness is one with the self, and that is the reason that justifies what Biko (1978) affirms as the righteousness of their strength. It is this strength that will write a new political script. It is the politics of those who are denied being, and in the face of this interdiction they radically insist on being free. Being as the locus of politics for Black Consciousness has much impact on how the world will be viewed, and since such a world is antiblack, how it will be confronted and combated. Gordon (2008, 91) states powerfully: 'Freedom continues to demand a face'.

Black Consciousness is the black coming to the self and thus embracing the very being of the black, as opposed to flying to the unconscious realm of being 'non-racial', 'post-racial' and 'race-denialist'. All these are acts of bad faith in response to the facticity of racism as the structure and infrastructure of the human condition. In affirming this facticity, Biko (1978, 50) writes: 'In terms of the Black Consciousness approach we recognise the existence of one major force in South Africa. This is White Racism'. It is clear what Black Consciousness is facing, and it is this force that it will be geared towards. White racism is a problem that creates antiblackness, and it is interlocked with all forms of systematic, systemic and continuing racist mechanics and machinations that will ensure that the status quo inaugurated by conquest will remain intact. This being-in-itself, as Sartre (1957, 62) notes, is the consciousness of 'here and now'. Consciousness comes from its own being. Black Consciousness, according to More (2017, 54), has been advocated by those who have been 'authentically acknowledging their blackness and began to define themselves accordingly'. It is a continued radical undertaking, a tradition of good faith – that is, being faithful to the existential conditions as they are and making means to confront them as they are, and calling them as they are. 'What is at stake is the power and authority to define' (More 2017, 55).

To conclude, the position of ante-Marx(ism) is decolonial in that it serves as the re-cartographization of the Azanian existential tradition, and of course, more broadly, the black radical tradition. The motif of these traditions is the principality of the imperative to exist. It is to insurgently insist on other modes of life in the face of fortified enclosure. It is to start from the position that existence, in a world gripped by dehumanization, is not a given. Therefore, it is just and justifiable to urgently engage in insurgency to exist. To cause insurrection, and thus resurrection, is the principal element of Biko's ante-Marx(ism) positionality – that is, to cultivate life as a domain of the *tabula rasa* and also the rubble that came from conquest. To think from that nothing and nothingness, the place of placelessness, that plane and plenitude of blackness which, in demanding that the world should have a human face, will continue to unmask that world.

What would it mean for this antiblack world to be ruptured by Azania?

Biko (1978, 70) asserts: 'We have to rewrite our history and describe in it the heroes that formed the core of resistance'. Ramose (1991, 25) affirms that 'the foundation of decolonization is the recognition and indeed the acceptance of the principle that the consequences of colonial conquest need to be reversed'. The demand for this reversal is dismissed out of hand as 'idealistic' and 'impractical'. This is the demand for life that must be restored by just means. And this means the absolute end of the racist-settler-colonialist-segregationist-apartheid-liberal-constitutionalist apparatus.

The principality of existence – the reparatory inscription of land, bread and humanity – marks Biko's *raison d'être*. This is the originary inscription of a liberated Azania.

In whose name Biko is speaking, in whose cause, and for whose life has been nothing but that spirited force that gives the gift of life. This, outside the humanist impulses that seek to defang Biko and render him a liberal humanist, has been his insistent drive to end this antiblack world, which from its making and markings of conquest has been a deathscape. Conquest has been a ferocious force that wages war against any form of life unless that life is capital itself. A different life-world has been the scariest gift of Azania that Biko, and the Azanian existential tradition before him, in his lifetime and in this afterlife, have been insisting on giving, while expecting no reciprocity – the gift of antagonism.

4 | Mabogo P. More's Intensifications

For the black to exist as liberated, there must be a different set of conditions that the black must create.

A question is worth posing: what, fundamentally, is at stake with regard to the black? There is a need for the black not only to be on a quest to explain the meaning of existence. Since the world is antiblack, and that is the dehumanizing structure and logic that fabricates the black's existence, the black has a duty to find and define the meaning of existence in terms that are its very own. It is the duty of the black, by the black, for the black, and in the name of the black to live in a liberated way and refuse to be used, misused and abused.

What is facing the black and what the black comes face-to-face with is dehumanization. The meaning of this fabricated force, institutionalized as reality even though it is not, should not only be falsified; rather, it should be unmasked and dismantled. For this to happen, there must be intensification. Simply put, intensification is a necessity – *what ought to be*. And it has been there throughout the long duration of the black's existential encounters and struggles since the idea of conquest was inaugurated as the order of the world – a world that came to be known as the antiblack world. From this disposition, intensification is a rallying point that animates Mabogo P. More's philosophical project. As a black disposition, it is the force that animates the black existential struggle. This force is the very constitutive element that brings something that is denied into being.

In his body of work, More pulls and pushes, depending on the force demanded by the situation that he deals with. As such, there is no stasis in his philosophical project. In pushing and pulling there is motion, acceleration and all discursive gestures that are on the move – and, of course, with intensity. Force is the way, but not the only way; it can be the right or the wrong way, depending on the situation in which it is exercised.

The mode of thinking black means that things must be different, and there must be a force in play to ensure that actualization of possibility comes into being to install a new set of conditions. If this is not done, there will be no change and things will remain as they are – in stasis. Deactualization is what comes as the result of stasis, and this means the mode of thinking black is not operative. There is nothing that happens, and nothing that is represented, relating to what should come into being as *what ought to be*.

What, then, to make of More? The intensification that animates him is clear from his non-conformism. He is a philosophical maverick and an intense philosopher. As a philosophical maverick, he pushes and pulls boundaries and unsettles philosophy, taking it out of its comfort zone and away from its absolutes. His mode of philosophizing is interruptive and awakening. Furthermore, he locates philosophy where it claims it is not supposed to be, as philosophy in black – that is, philosophy entrenched in things that are fallaciously claimed to be non-philosophical. Added to this, he scandalizes philosophy by exposing it to its own racist dealings and their dissimulations. As an intense philosopher, More challenges forces of dehumanization and charts a path for liberation, even if it is refused by those who oppress and dehumanize the black. From the contours of these claims, it is clear that the lived experience of the black demands a philosopher who is not only attuned to the black condition, but is able to tease out all forces of dehumanization through diagnosis, and excavate the underlying meaning of things that inform dehumanization in intense ways, deploying both rigour and fidelity to *what ought to be.*

Clearly, being a maverick and making intense demands exhaust all means at the disposal of a philosopher in times of reckoning. More's philosophical contribution is an original one. And the stakes are very high for his philosophy, given the nature of the unforgiving antiblack world. The exhaustive nature of his philosophical acts lies in the paradox of suspension of the commonly held beliefs and exposition – unmasking – of what is concealed, saying what is censored, which are taken up in unison as contradictory forces and operationalized not only to give meaning but to make meaning. The disposition of suspension and exposition, seen from the position of the black, clearly gives way to an understanding of Black Consciousness. What then emerges is the intensification through which suspension and exposition create protocols that will install the agenda of the pursuit of liberation. A disposition that is enunciated from a principled position, one which will be in favour or disfavour depending on what is being stood for in terms of the breaking open of a path, that militancy against enclosure, is something that is not missing when philosophy is on a mission and is armed with a clear agenda. Such philosophy, philosophy in black, means having a clear agenda. The articulation and the expression of this agenda, the denied ones altering their fate, is intensification. The grammar of philosophy in black means standing *for something, in something, with something.* The aspirations of liberation become apparent if there is that agenda, that force.

There is, in More's philosophical opus, that intensification. His philosophical project is philosophy in black. It is that project that runs against the grain. Not that it is difference for its own sake, but that it enacts the very standing the black assumes as a result of being denied humanity, and actualizes the possibility that opposes this denial. For this dissenting standing to be assumed, it must be based on the refusal to be interpellated and hegemonized, to be complicit in dehumanization. This intensification is a force that stands against all forms of dehumanization. In articulation and expression, it can be said to be everything that is philosophically black, the meaning of existence in so far as black philosophy is concerned – that is, philosophy in black. The project of black existence, or existence of blackness, cannot be something that is thought outside the question of being. More's itinerary does not turn back and wallow in apologia; it is a clear agenda, and what infuses it is the mission to ensure that the existential conditions of the black should be fundamentally different from what they are in an antiblack world.

A force of critique

Truly, in More's philosophy there lies a vital force of critique against dehumanization of the black. The force dispatches this critique through the assertion of humanity. Even if this humanity is denied, it is willed through the elevation of Black Consciousness philosophy. This intensification, as More wills it, means mapping the contours of existence. Black Consciousness philosophy means the black necessarily coming to the self on its own terms to confront and combat dehumanization. And the black self will emerge in its own image where consciousness is transacted among those who rally around the cause of their suffering to cultivate their own sense of self, not the one that is fabricated by antiblack racism. The envisaged self, even during defeat, is willed and thus actualized to create a different set of conditions. Black Consciousness philosophy is a force, the consistent agenda, that *standing* of More. It is, more fundamentally, phenomenology's ethical task, and that is to insist on *what ought to be*. And it is, in a sense, an ethical task that More takes to be responsible for responsibility itself. By this is meant that philosophy is concerned with the lived reality, experience and facticity not only of being-in-the-world but of being-black-in-an-antiblack-world. This black condition demands an understanding of dehumanization, and it is from this understanding that More's philosophy derives its force as Africana existential phenomenology, whose unique disposition is being concerned not with generality, but with the being and specific lived experience of the black-in-an-antiblack-world. It is not only the meaning of existence that is of concern to More, but how a different set of conditions can be brought into being to inaugurate the rupture of liberation.

The refusal to concede, to be complicit, and to be in the double bind of ambivalence about antiblack racism for fear of upsetting whites, thus indecisive and prone to betrayal, is what separates force from submission. What arises from this force is choice: not only being chosen, but exercising choice with all might – that is to say, intensification. Intensification is justified by the condition of being denied the free exercise of choice, even in the face of unfreedom or the very absence of that choice. More's philosophy in black is the intensification that confronts dehumanization; as a project, it means dwelling in politics, thus insisting that there is always a way through or out.

Philosophy and politicization

But then, why does More demand intensification? Well, he has the answer. 'In this context, the philosopher surpasses philosophical speculation and becomes one with the activity of philosophising through her intense involvement with the problems at hand' (More 2017, 76). Philosophy here is a politicized enterprise; it is, so to say, the existential phenomenological project in its radical form in that it is an 'intense involvement'. It is not a 'contemplative approach', as More (2017, 76) warns, detached from the lived reality of the world. By calling this philosophy Africana philosophy, More is making a crucial point about intensification in that this is the philosophy that deals with the existential problematics of being-black-in-an-antiblack-world. It is an intense philosophy that is rightly and justifiably concerned with and occupied by the problem of racism. Thus, intensification is not a luxurious muse, but a necessary and fundamental task. For racism in its antiblack nature is there to dehumanize, and that is what causes those who are philosophizing to take up this task, because their humanity is brought into question.

Having heard enough of antiblack racism, and thus stating 'enough is enough', their attitude is formed from the stance of the black experiential world gripped by antiblackness. Where the black is prohibited and criminalized, the typical imposition of the antiblack oppressive state apparatus, there will be no concession made to submit to this absurdity. In fact, for the black, politics is life, and there is no way that the black will submit to being denied the will to live. This is not a right but a force of might, an intensification. To say that the black should stay out of politics is to say that the black should not be responsible for its own being. For More, philosophy cannot stay out of politics and wallow in complicity, where politics are branded as the activity of the oppressive state and philosophy is just a matter of mental exercise and pure abstraction. The philosophical reflection that has to do with being-in-the-world cannot be detached from politics. According to

Steve Biko (1978, 27), politics cannot be engaged with from 'a detached point of view' but from what is forever urgent, the point of view of the black. This black point of view is the one whose intensification More calls for. It is what comes into being as the result of conviction. Understanding what intensification is means the radical emphasizing of the point of view of the black, despite the sanctions of the oppressive state apparatus.

This is made explicit by Biko through Black Consciousness philosophy. By way of an operational definition, he writes:

> Briefly defined therefore, Black Consciousness is in essence the realisation by the black man [sic] of the need to rally together with his brothers [sic] around the cause of their operation – the blackness of their black skin – and operate as a group in order to rid themselves of shackles that bind them to perpetual servitude. It seeks to demonstrate the lie that black is an aberration from the 'normal' which is white. (Biko 1978, 49)

More (2017) registers Black Consciousness philosophy as *what ought to be*, and that as a political project essentially means it is decolonization. Black Consciousness, thus defined as a way of life, is the necessity of a livable life as desired by the black. It is the politics that are animated by intensification. 'It emphasizes the awareness of the power of the black self to free itself from everything oppressive' (More 2017, 75). To add to this, Chabani Manganyi (1977, 54) submits that 'in the case of South Africa, the black consciousness movement of identity retrieval and creation emerged as the *antithesis* of the white dominant culture'. This antithesis is intensification, because the black rejected what the white imposed and affirmed what the black itself asserted. This

111

standing, this standing for something, is the radical political act, gesture and signature. That is why, for Manganyi, it becomes a mode of imprinting, a mark. For it is propelled by the desire *to be*, which is coupled with *what ought to be*. Black Consciousness is, according to Manganyi (1977, 54), a 'profound need in the inner world of the black collective psyche to materialize a new identity to harness all the resources of cultural and historical unconscious'. It is to reshape the self, and also reshape the manner in which the energy and drive of the black are repurposed to fulfil the way of being in politics.

To be involved in politics does not necessarily mean to be inside politics, even though there can seem to be no variation between these two positions. But it is important to highlight that one can be involved in politics without being fully responsible for such politics. While being involved in politics, one can opt out of responsibility for them. But to be inside politics is not only a matter of being involved. It is to be the self that is politics – *to be politics, to be political*. It is not only being identified with politics, but being the figure of politics, that thing that is seen by the state as the being who should stay out of politics. This prohibition is imposed on the black. In an antiblack world, the dehumanization of the black is expected to go unquestioned and what should prevail is a climate of fear and silence; and when the black stands up, the prohibition is imposed to make the black stay out of politics (More 1996).

So, to be inside politics is an ethical task that More (2017), as a philosopher, a black one at that, doing philosophy in black, radically insists on. It is intensification that serves as evidence that he has made, makes and will make a mark through what he calls 'a *radical philosophy*' (More 2017, 78, emphasis in the original). The philosophical outlook of these politics had to come from the black through the philosophical project called

Black Consciousness. More's philosophical project, one which is enunciated from the position of being black, and that project being black in its disposition, is the rearticulation of politics. In its register, it is both necessity and possibility. Intensification is coined by More as a praxis.

> It is this movement from thinking to acting that makes Black Consciousness philosophy a *radical philosophy*. It enjoins its adherent's reflection (theory), the acting is aimed at political and social action. Together, theory and praxis are fundamentally connected to the rational utopia (what ought-to-be), with changing, altering or transforming society. (More 2017, 78, emphasis in the original)

More's call for philosophy's task to be politicized in relation to the question of the being of the black, particularly being-black-in-an-antiblack-world, lies at the heart of his philosophical project, his intensification. And the philosophical arena in which he will be located and grounded, for the purposes of this meditation, is Black Consciousness philosophy, which

> was and still is a struggle for a new consciousness, a reawakening of a self-consciousness, a re-appropriation of black self-consciousness from the clutches of an appropriative and dominating white consciousness, a rediscovery of the black self which lay buried beneath white consciousness imposed on blacks by cultural, political, economic, linguistic and religious domination. (More 2004, 86)

Part of the reason is that *what ought to be* is clearly insisted upon not as a generality, but as the specificity of changing the antiblack world into a liberated world, the obliteration of dehumanization *tout court*. This, in Black Consciousness philosophy, is intensification's imperative. And this intensification is justified because the antiblack is so grand and petty, just like the apartheid that Biko (1978) emphatically declared to be evil.

The meaning of being

The meaning of being is intensified. Here is a question: what is the meaning of being-in-the-world? This is an important and general question. But due to the situation that More is dealing with, he poses a more pertinent question, a fundamental one as the stakes are high: what is the meaning of being-black-in-an-antiblack-world? Of course, these two questions are rooted in existential phenomenology, but it is worth noting the intensification that comes with the latter question. In fact, the particularity and specificity of this question makes it a fitting one for Black Consciousness philosophy, and in particular, for More's philosophical project. This is phenomenology's intensification. The question does not come out of the blue, it is rooted in the lived experience of being black, and thus denied humanity. 'That Black Consciousness refers to a form of *consciousness* already calls for a phenomenological analysis' (Gordon 2008, 83, emphasis in the original).

What happens also, on another level, is what Lewis Gordon (2008, 87) writes of as the organization of meaning that comes into being as a 'discursive opposition'. Since Black Consciousness is intensification, clearly its discursive opposition does not sit well with the apartheid regime. For, it being politics proper, it serves, according to Gordon (2008, 87), 'the role of politics in the context of political formation'. It is this formation that is banned. The inseparability of necessity and possibility clearly shows that Black Consciousness philosophy is, politically *strictu sensu*, a force on which the racist apartheid state is willing to declare war.

As a result of this condition, politics become a radical formation, and for More (2012), these are the politics of being, which means the inseparability of politics and ontology. In Black Consciousness philosophy, More argues, existential ontology and politics are symbiotic. This is about, if anything at all, 'the politics of being in an antiblack world' (More 2012, 24). So the politics of being are accountable to the ontological facticity of the black who is in the black condition (More 2012). It is from this condition that More's philosophical project, which can also be called the Azanian existential phenomenological inscription, stems. In dealing with this naked form of dehumanization, More (2014, 3) states that Azanian existential phenomenology deals with 'a fundamentally deep and complex oppressive system'. Having referred to apartheid only in terms of its breadth and depth as a phenomenon, what about the forces that precede and animate apartheid? Clearly, it is impossible for his project to phenomenologically exhaust the long history of dehumanization. However, the attempt is made in his phenomenology to inscribe the meaning of being-black-in-an-antiblack-world throughout this history. At issue is what More (2012, 26) refers to as the fundamental 'topic of what it means to be human'. His project is what people are, in a real sense. And with specific reference to the black, in the condition of being dehumanized by having one's humanity called into question, the topic of what it means to be human is not a given. The denial of the humanity of the black makes this topic a subject of interrogation.

More's intensification is at the epicentre of his philosophical project. Even in this contemporary moment marked as post-1994 South Africa, the political fault lines still run deep. This is what the black condition is, and clearly, where the black is, in the abyss, is the pit that Black Consciousness stems from, and it is where the idea of Azania is birthed. The *longue durée* of

115

dehumanization, that overarching span of what can be called an era, period, or epoch, is deep time, the longevity that is beyond comprehension. There is no radical break, as the so-called 'post-' or 'aftermath' of that *longue durée* is a radical continuity with it.

Azania gives primacy to the restoration of the black being, settling due reparations, returning stolen land, and absolute destruction and uprooting of racism in its types and variations. Complete exorcism of the spirit of this *longue durée* will bring a different conception of the black world in freedom, the spirit that is in line with 'keeping the light of hope alive' (More 2017, 32). This is because Azania has been incubated in the tragic times of this *longue durée* of dehumanization, but it has been a dream that will never die.

Intensification against liberal conformism

Pandering to the liberal sensibilities that appeal to the 'voice of reason', or asking for someone to be reasonable, is what More subjects to 'a grand refusal to forget', as Jeremy Glick (2016, 1) notes, that refusal to wallow in amnesia. The terms of struggle are dictated by the black. The phenomenological project will, charting the path to liberation, have to examine not only the content of this grammar, but its intensification. This demands a concerted effort to understand what is fundamentally at stake in so far as dehumanization is concerned. To call into question the stakes the black faces in mounting the ethos and possibility of liberation means there is no way that dehumanization can be disavowed. Liberation, for the black, is enunciated from the position of being denied a way of being alive, and this assertion of being alive is the very constitutive element of More's intensification. It is not that life is a given; it is created with intention and intensity. By positioning philosophy as the radical force, as intensification, what emerges is what Frank Wilderson (2008b, 99) calls a 'grammar of suffering' – that is, the incommunicable coming to language, and thus saying the unsayable. This, of course, will not sit well with the liberal grammar that claims to be the absolute and the universal, under the guise of reason. For it to claim reason is for it to regulate and absolutely control the black; the black must remain forever mute, and, if speaking is permitted, it will be a guided speech. Everything that falls outside the liberal grip is considered unreasonable, and that means there must be conformism, the very thing that More rejects *in toto*.

The liberation of the black will not be guided by liberal conformism, which is there to fortify dehumanization. Even its telos, according to Frantz Fanon (1967), is nothing other than everything that has always been misleading. Fanon points to different forms of life, and these forms are essential in under-standing the misleading nature of liberal conformism as well as More's non-conformism. Fanon (1967, 220) highlights the distinction in having gone 'from one way of life to another, but not from one life to another'. One way of life, which has been mastered by liberal conformism, the exterior of the conscious-ness of the black, black alienation, raises the expectation that comes with believing in cosmetic change. 'Apparently it's alright with the liberals as long as you remain caught by *their* trap' (Biko 1978, 25). It is this misleading nature that enables the pretence that there is real change taking place, whereas it is only cosmetic. 'Instead it requires the admission of the fact that fundamentally the situation doesn't have to be as it is' (More 2014, 7). Fanon warns of the pitfalls of this way of life in which the black, being susceptible, is the one who 'suffers a relapse' (Fanon 1967, 220); this way of life is a fatal one, as per Wilderson's remark (2008b, 99) that 'Blackness suffers through the homology of Absence'. This absence, of course, is that of not having any ontological presence. Put differently, the black is absented from the domain of humanity and that is why dehumanization reigns. By being denied humanity, Wilderson writes, 'Blacks cannot *be*' (2008b, 98, emphasis in the original). It is not the life that the black fought for itself, and, in terms of liberation, it is not liberation because it does not bring with it fundamental changes, only cosmetic ones. As such, liberal conformism appropriates it. Fanon delivers an exposé:

> But the Negro knows nothing of the cost of freedom, for he has not fought for it. From time to time he has fought for Liberty and Justice, but these were always white liberty and white justice; that is, values secreted by his masters. (Fanon 1967, 221)

But then, what to make of what Fanon calls the radical opposite of this? Fanon makes mention of moving 'from one life to another' which, for Black Consciousness, has been the firm locus, the life of the black as determined by the black – in short, the life that has been oppressed but which has not submitted to the forces of the liberal consensus. The ontology of Black Consciousness, as More shows, is the one which stood firm against liberal conformism and which, in its philosophical intensification, led to the expulsion of liberals. It is this expulsion that Manganyi (1973, 17) coins as 'putting the liberals out of work'. It is this intensification that led adherents of Black Consciousness, and to a large extent any black who stands up for her or his liberation, to be accused of being ungrateful. Radically insisting on the Fanonesque 'from one life to another' means seeking fundamental change, and no longer letting the black be used. The daring stance taken by Black Consciousness is the animating force of More's phenomenological inscription, which will not fall under the spell of the liberal consensus. For this grand refusal to be in operation there should be intensification, because the liberal agenda will stop at nothing to confuse, obstruct and corrupt the efforts to achieve black liberation.

Manganyi (1973, 17) writes: 'This kind of reaction is not entirely unexpected when one considers that South African liberalism can only be a form of narcissism – a form of self-love. People who love themselves can pity only themselves, hardly anybody else'. The liberal rage is nothing but narcissism.

> These self-appointed trustees of black interest boast of years of experience in their fight for the 'rights of blacks'. They have been doing things for blacks, on behalf of blacks, and because of blacks. When the blacks announce that the time has come for them to do things for themselves and all by themselves all white liberals shout blue murder! (Biko 1978, 25)

The liberal will not feel good to see the black liberated. The liberation of the black, for sure, soils the liberal's 'pious work', as expressed by Manganyi (1973, 17) – that is, the banal cry that the black has forgotten the absolute good that the liberal has done. This cry does not emerge out of sincerity, and it is not only insincere but insensitive. Well, sincerity and sensitivity are non-existent traits of the narcissist. The narcissist could not care less if there is black suffering. If there is suffering, clearly, that must be ended by the black, acting in accord with their own will. But the narcissist will not allow the black to act to end their suffering. This would make the narcissist irrelevant. The narcissist feels good when holding a firm grip on the black and subjecting the black to the spell of liberal conformism. This conformism does not emerge out of a dialogue. The narcissist's communicative gesture is a monologue. Fanon (1967, 221) is right here: 'But most often there is nothing – nothing but indifference, or a paternalistic curiosity'. The narcissism of the liberal, in its lust and drive to invalidate the black sense of being and actionality that results from acting from the situation of antiblackness, amounts to sadism. The liberal derives enjoyment from black suffering. Put differently: white privilege is amassed by black dispossession. The sadist derives pleasure from the pain of the Other. The sadist does not see the Other as a sentient being, but as a thing. The sadist, Jean-Paul Sartre avers (1965, 49), is at heart 'a criminal'. The dehumanization drive of the sadist is captured by Paulo Freire (1994, 42) thus: 'The oppressed, as objects, as "things", have no purposes except those their oppressors prescribe for them'. The liberal claims to act on behalf of the black, and thus to exercise absolute control over the black bodily being; this is the consumptive drive of sadism.

> Sadistic love is perverted love – a love of death, not life. One of the characteristics of the oppressor consciousness and its necrophilic view of the world is thus sadism. As the oppressor consciousness, in order to dominate, tries to deter the drive to search, the restlessness, and the creative power which characterize life, it kills life. (Freire 1994, 42)

The killing of life is, as Sartre (1965) says, the sadist's pure function, in that the sadist is always making preparations for death, but only if it is the death of the Other. Even though the sadist might not express this murderous drive openly, the explicit drive is replaced with the implicit one. Here is a damning verdict on all sadists, which Sartre (1965, 49) delivers in emphatic terms:

'They are symbolic murderers'. That is why it is clear, in More's philosophy, that the liberal qua sadist is antithetical to liberation. Freedom, equality and justice are abstractions, not concrete conditions, when it comes to the black who confronts antiblack racism. As Fanon (1967) shows, these are values that have nothing to do with the liberation of the black. What, then, should prevail? The black must remain a white object for the liberal, a thing. The black should not be the being-in-itself or being qua being. The black must always be what the liberal desires. That is why when the black exercises liberation through Black Consciousness the liberal goes on the defensive and the offensive by way of narcissistic rage. More (2005, 220) presents this scandal thus: 'The liberal is, as a matter of fact, an in-the-closet assimilationist, one who wants blacks to be full members of humanity (read white) only if they renounce their blackness'. Biko (1978, 64) calls this a myth, one which should be 'cracked' and 'killed'. There lies Biko's intensification. It is what More (2017, 15) calls 'rejection': claiming authenticity in order thereby to be free from bad faith. 'Authentic being-black-in-the-world necessitated liberation from the terror of fear and death' (More 2017, 15). Intensification is necessitated and justified by the will to be liberated. This liberation is authenticity; it is informed by the black existential struggle and refusal to be acted upon by the white liberal. It is only in inauthenticity that the white liberal will have the upper hand over the black.

The liberal has been the purveyor of the myth of assimilating the black so that the black will be what the liberal wants. The black cannot be a real self, only the artefact of the liberal. This makes the liberal what Albert Memmi (1965, 70) calls the 'benevolent colonizer' who claims to be on the side of blacks but is in fact an oppressor. This figure of the benevolent colonizer is, according to Sartre (1965, 55), what comes to be called 'a democrat', one who is labelled a 'feeble protector'. But the liberal is not at all a protector, if such protection is said to be extended to the black. According to Memmi (1965, 43), 'the benevolent colonizer can never attain the good, for his only choice is not between good and evil, but between evil and uneasiness'. That is why the liberal is invested in keeping the status quo intact. For Sartre (1965), the liberal fears any elevation of consciousness in those whom he claims to protect, because then they will exist on their own and determine their own cause. To talk about the liberal and the democrat is, in fact, to talk about the figure of bad faith, already examined in chapter 3. Sartre (1957, 70) amplifies this as follows: 'Bad faith seeks by means of "not-being-what-one-is" to escape from the in-itself which I am not in the mode of being what one is not. It denies itself as bad faith and aims at the in-itself which I am not in the mode of "not-being-what-one-is-not"'. Gordon (1995, 8) operationalizes bad faith as fleeing 'a displeasing truth for a pleasing falsehood'. Here, More (2017, 91) offers a lucid illumination: 'In simple terms, bad faith is a form of self-deception, consciously lying to itself about its freedom'. And Nelson Maldonado-Torres (2008b, 120) states that 'lying to oneself also involves the denial of choice in the face of different possibilities'.

Sartre (1957) notes how bad faith is antithetical and even lethal to any human project. For the human project is being-towards-freedom, the very project that bad faith is antithetical towards, even to the extent of utterly denying it. And this is because bad faith is the denial of humanity. It is the fabrication of facticity. 'Bad faith apprehends evidence, but it is resigned in advance to not being fulfilled by this evidence, to not being persuaded and transformed into good faith' (Sartre 1957, 68). Bad faith is the contamination of any project that has to do with liberation, what Sartre calls the 'pursuit of Being' (1957, xix). Bad faith is, in its fabricated structure, a 'firm resolution', as Sartre states. 'The true problem of bad faith stems evidently from the fact that bad faith is *faith*' (1957, 67, emphasis in the original). And the spirit of bad faith is what underwrites the existence of the liberal. According to Memmi,

> the distance between his commitment and that of the colonized will have unforeseen and insurmountable consequences. Despite his attempts to take part in the politics of the colony, he will be constantly out of step in his language and in his actions. He might hesitate or reject a demand of the colonized, the significance of which he will not immediately grasp. This lack of perception will seem to confirm his indifference. (Memmi 1965, 42)

The liberal is always in bad faith and in the antiblack world; as More (2005, 216) states, 'bad faith is endemic'. The black who believes in being acted upon by the white liberal, not knowing the cost of freedom and believing in the false generosity of the liberal, is acting in bad faith since this is not liberation. To be within Black Consciousness, to be the being who intensifies *what ought to be*, is to act in good faith. In More's existential phenomenological articulation, Black Consciousness is a determination of being black in the world. As such, it is the will of the black, and it falls upon the black to fight for liberation.

The gift of the self to the self
When the one who is known as not having fought for liberation starts to do so, to act without any liberal paternalism, it is not surprising to hear liberals expose their narcissistic rage and

proclaim how ungrateful the black is. To the pious work that liberals have been claiming as their act of prudence and sagacity, Sartre (1964, 24) would retort as follows: 'I never stopped creating myself; I was both giver and gift'. This is the intensification that the liberal cannot stand. The liberal does not want the black to bestow the gift upon itself, to be a gift – that is, the gift of *the self to the self*, the generous gift. For Freire (1994, 43), this is liberation and it 'requires a profound rebirth'. There lies More's intensification.

It is a generous gift as it is given without any expectation, despite the intensified force that animates it. The liberal's narcissistic rage attests to the fact that there is nothing worthy of a gift in the 'pious work' that Manganyi (1973) exposes liberals as guilty of. This, in point of fact, demands attention to what Freire (1994, 26) calls 'false charity', which is dispossession where the 'oppressors must perpetuate injustice as well'. The perpetuation of injustice will go on unabated because false charity, which is merely cosmetic change, is seen as a gift while it is really dispossession. More (2011, 174) warns that 'the gift of humanhood without a struggle still constitutes the slave as a slave since he/she has not attained independent self-consciousness and thus remains dominated by the master'. Liberation, in its genuine nature, will be compromised, and everything will be at the expense of the black. More (2011, 174) is opposed to the liberation that 'emerges from without and not from within the slave', for it will always be in favour of oppression and not liberation. The intensification that Freire calls profound rebirth should, by all means, serve as the indicative force showing that those who emerge are of that Fanonian stock – that is, those who have moved 'from one life to another' – with a different conception of life altogether. This is the fundamental change that comes as the result of intensification. 'Those who undergo it must take on a

new form of existence; they can no longer remain as they were'
(Freire 1994, 43).

In the position of strength, that potent force, lies More's
grand refusal in the name of Black Consciousness. As phenomenology's radical project, Black Consciousness brings into being
a different set of conditions. Intensification leads to rupture. It is
not a negotiated settlement, which, for More (2011), is rooted in
the epistemology of pacifists and legalists. From their disposition,
obviously not wanting to rock the boat, there will be no rupture.
All measures should be moderate. But this moderation does not
mean the middle ground, it means keeping the status quo intact.
This is what makes Fanon (1965) call for the severing of colonial
ties, and this severance is acutely present in Black Consciousness's
expulsion of liberals from black affairs. For, as Biko (1978, 25)
writes, 'the blacks have heard enough of this'. By insisting on
being involved in the fight for liberation (paternalistically so) the
liberal is not only contaminating this fight waged by the black. For
Fanon (1965, 180), it 'could always be read as a token of an indefi-
nite oppression'. And this should not be taken lightly as implying a
possibility; it is *what is*, the *thing itself*. To say the 'token' is to say the
real thing. Against this, Fanon emphasizes intensification.

> We have reviewed the victorious progress of the
> colonized on the path of his liberation, as revealed in
> the number of particular aspects. We have indicated
> that strictly on the level of the individual and his
> tremendous dynamism a revolution – fundamental,
> irreversible, ever more far-reaching – has occurred.
> (Fanon 1965, 180)

The intensification that More (2011) mounts is one that pacifists and legalists cannot stall. It is the intensification that, in its

Fanonian fold, is liberation, and that is what the black fights for. Liberation is not a telos, but what is in the making.

> The explosion will not happen today. It is too soon . . . or too late.
>
> I do not come with timeless truths.
>
> My consciousness is not illuminated with ultimate radiances.
>
> Nevertheless, in complete composure, I think it would be good if certain things were said. (Fanon 1967, 7)

In the exploratory quest for what the black wants, Fanon does not chain liberation to a telos. There is work at hand, and this work being informed by the telos of *what ought to be*, More (2004, 83) states that it requires blacks to know what they are (coming to consciousness and engaging in Black Consciousness) and 'to discover what we ought to be doing'. More's intensification gives meaning to this work by going beyond what is known and anticipated to include other, unknown possibilities as well. It is an animating force whose experimental nature shows its rootedness in Black Consciousness philosophy. According to More (2004, 89), Black Consciousness is 'a means towards freedom rather than an end in itself', the animating force that drives *what ought to be* – that is, intensification as it radically unfolds in antagonism and combat against antiblackness – and he avers (2004, 97) that 'there is at a deeper level the means/ends problem that finds expression in the antithetical/synthetical moments at play'.

It is this intensification that makes the struggle for liberation an enduring one. No easy solutions are sought. What is expressed is a radical critique whose affirmative register attends to what the black wants – and the black wants to be liberated.

In this means/ends problematic, the black does not ask to be acted upon. The black is, in itself, responsible for its freedom. The black in Black Consciousness is expressing what has been deemed incommunicable. There is no way that the anticipatory counter-utterance can be a deputized speech, what Fanon (1965, 172) calls 'sweet-sister speech', one that is laced with bad faith as it takes flight from saying things as they are. In More's intensifications, the things that Fanon says must be expressed with that form of radical insistence – for they are nothing but necessity itself. And they carry within them critique; hence liberation is a critical project. More's intensifications are such a project. The trial and error that happens during the exercise of thought in struggle, the phenomenological radical project, enunciated from the position of being-black-in-an-antiblack-world, makes intensification the very conduit of liberation. The critique of the colonial project comes through this phenomenological radical project, this intensification of critique. To this extent, everything in this disposition is direct in that it initiates a face-to-face encounter. More does not mask his face as he continues to face the colonial mask, antiblackness, whose consciousness is that of bad faith. Liberation has been intensified and continues to be intensified in good faith.

But this does not mean that the black is proving that it is in good faith in order to initiate a dialogue with antiblackness. In this regard, the black is in good faith with itself and for itself. This is what Black Consciousness is, hence its dictum that the black is on its own. This means that everything is wholly dependent on the black. More's intensification as phenomenology's radical project is the making of the world that results from the radical efforts of the black, and not from the world that is given to the black. The latter is not the world but the antiblack world. The powerful voice is the edifice of Black Consciousness, and there is, in the moments of the quest for liberation, the rallying cry to be free. 'Liberation therefore, is of paramount importance in the concept of Black Consciousness, for we cannot be conscious of ourselves and yet remain in bondage. We want to attain the envisioning self which is a free self' (Biko 1978, 49). It is the free world that is being cried out for. It is the world that, in its radical conception, is the rallying cry of Black Consciousness – where the black will exist as a being and not a thing. It is this existence in which, having named oneself, liberated oneself and defined oneself *as black*, as Black Consciousness, that liberation can be installed. This installation is, according to More's intensification, a necessary task that cannot be left outside the firm grasp and heightened sense of consciousness of the black, both of which require philosophical commitment and engagement to realize liberation even in the condition of failure.

Intensification without end

More's intensification is the beginning of no end. The radical unfolding of his philosophical gesture causes prescriptions and predictions to fail. Since the liberation that has been and continues to be fought for has not been attained, things are not coming to a close. Instead, there are more radical openings. Black Consciousness philosophy, the radical inscription authorizing the black being, the way that traces the path of a detour (the always unfamiliar route), is, in More's intensifications, by way of liberation – radically committed to the task at hand, and coming face-to-face with what conceals, and thus abandoning fear in all of its hesitant and paralyzing manifestations.

More is wedded to the existential struggle of the black, and his philosophical activity is an intense philosophy; the disposition of philosophy in black is the concrete manifestation of this. It is the philosophical project that deals with the problems of existence from the lived experience of being-black-in-an-antiblack-world, in particular from the disposition of philosophy in black. It is not that existence is naturally problematic in itself; what is problematic is the existence that has been fabricated and the one that the black sets out to change fundamentally.

Intensification mobilizes and advances. This active force does not stand active all the time, but it being at times exhausted and demobilized does not translate into its radical failure. It is intensification in that it is the indomitable will not only to endure, but to continuously create, even out of nothing. It is, in short, always a matter of necessity. There lies the generative spirit of intensification. It is not the testament of its age, or of having been reduced to claiming relevance. The quest to exist, to de/form the world, that access, accent and ascent to being otherwise, is where the generative inscription lies. The phenomenological inscription, that writerly force, writing what the black likes, in that animated spirit of Black Consciousness, there lies More's philosophical genius. The inscriptive code insists on writing what is denied – not only at the level of content, or because of the denial of the writerly being of the black – to make its consciousness the rallying phenomenological project. This radical insistence is coupled with the heightened spirit of refusal, the refusal to be the possession of what is exterior to the black self. Drawing from the existential ruins of the black as the site of creative potential, intensification comes as the radical gift that is not only the object of exchange, but the generator of life itself – however denied. The authentic quest for the human spirit, the authenticity of More's critical good faith, is what causes the existential struggle to elucidate meaning to be an ongoing one, as part of phenomenology's critical task of making a case for the investigation of the lived experience of being-black-in-an-antiblack-world. There is a way that operates differently from the known; it is not the only way, but, as per More's existential detour from enclosure, it operates *by way of liberation*. This is what the different set of conditions for the existence of the black is all about, it is *that way*.

Postscript | The 'X-File' (Notes on Extended Thought)

The image of the black is ubiquitous.
—Anthony P. Farley, 'The Poetics of Colorlined Space'

What if this is the beginning? Or is there an end to speak of in the realm of thought?

Since thought is infinite, what is presented is *that* file, a specific kind of file whose form and content will be generated as part of an investigation into the concept of thought itself. The propensity to think, from the extended disposition that takes the black point of view as a critical discursive site, means the beginning unfolds in figurative and literal forms.

Here is the file. The X-File is the X, of X, written and compiled by X, and from X's disposition. This, of course, is not a mediated form. In a sense, it is X's thought, composition and expression – a black point of view contra conquest.

The X-File contains what should be disclosed. It has nothing to do with secrecy. In the face of what renders secrecy, the idea of the sacred, the X-File is the unsealing of that.

This file contains side or marginal notes that sprang forth in the unfolding of thought. The tenor of this file is theoretical in form. It is the file which, in loose terms, can be declared to mean extended thought. This is its content in the context of having to think against conquest.

The X-File is an ongoing investigation, that radical opening which comes in the form of rupture. This gives way to interstices. The pressure point intensifies to rupture at the interstice where thought emerges against the despotic order of meaning, to produce other meanings. The interstices, according to Roland Barthes (1982), signify a perforation of the surface. X, then, is this perforation. As Barthes (1982, 24) articulates it, this is 'a purely interstitial object' which he links with emptiness. But when X is thrown into the fold, there is a whole reconfiguration taking place in that X is not that interstitial object, but the force that makes that interstitial object exist. In other words, the inscription of X denotes that force which causes the interstitial marks to be seen on the surface, and these become cracks that are pushed further until rupture continually unfolds. The interstices, according to Hortense Spillers (2003), mark the origin of X not only as an inscription but as speech. This is where rupture is located. 'The missing word – the interstice – both as that which allows us to speak about and that enables us to speak at all – shares, in this case, a common border with another country of symbols – the iconographic' (Spillers 2003, 156). There has forever been that apparatus of violence that has been charged directly with erasing thought from the domain of the black, through what Spillers marks as 'imagistic absences'. This has been met with the resistant force of the black, thinking from its own point of view and in its own name, X. The black must deal with authorizing itself in the midst of de-authorizations. These absences are what Barthes (1982, 24) sees as the 'clump of emptiness, a collection of perforations'. But there is a push for the closure of the interstices so that X does not emerge. 'Consequently, the banished place and the banished person acquire an element of secrecy, and discourse about them is circumscribed and coded' (Spillers 2003, 165). The clandestine circulation of life, among those who are in the chokehold of antiblackness, comes to mean the life of those who insist on existing. By way of extending this thought, the question is about the ways in which the black point of view becomes manifest.

Stated clearly, extended thought is the black having its own conception of being – the blackness of being, as David Marriott (2018a) states, that which becomes a better conception of the self in relation to the world that must be created through the existential struggle; thus, the black as the definer of its terms. This does not wallow in 'coalition politics' that include the black and where these terms are managed by liberal conformism. Instead, the call is for the form and content of expression that have nothing to do with the politics of legibility, recognition and respectability. There is no need for the black to ingratiate itself with whiteness. Frank Wilderson (2020, 12) emphasizes the break of blackness from the 'unconscious consensus', and states that the black, as X, should institute its own modes of discourse as opposed to being reduced to those of 'sentient implements'.

The meta-aporia of Azania

The X of blackness, then, in this form, stands for what goes deeper than what Jacques Derrida (1993) coins as aporia, which is the state of undecidability brought about by contradictions in the realm of the textual and discourse. At issue is something wholly different. For X, it is worth following 'a meta-aporia for political thought and action' (Wilderson 2020, 13). In a different line of abstraction, opposing Derrida, Wilderson (2020, 14, emphasis in the original) argues that meta-aporia for X is 'not one topic *of* discussion but *discussion itself*'. Having noted that Azania is the place where X is, and where thinking, knowing and doing are litigated and liquidated by the idea of South Africa with what Wilderson (2020, 12) terms 'unconscious consensus', there is a counterforce at play, the black point of view. This point of view is the constitutive element of meta-aporia, as Wilderson coins it. Meta-aporia means Azania is a discussion itself, it is discourse proper. This, certainly, is the word and world of Azania. X excavates meta-aporias, to expose narratives of 'redemption', which for Wilderson (2020, 16) are nothing but what serves a parasitic function that feeds on the black. It is the black who embraces X, to break from the 'unconscious consensus' that makes this parasitic function go unchecked.

This is an elaboration of a practice in germane and generative ways. The distilling of X, it also being a force of distillation, the double operation deployed, insists on the reconfiguring of the word and the world as inseparable from each other. X is not out there to be a corrective tool, or what explains itself in order to be clutched by accommodationist forces that pervade the idea of South Africa within the 'unconscious consensus'. X does not justify itself by blinding itself to the logics of what Marriott (2018a, 57) calls 'a racist semiology'. The latter is what pervades the idea of South Africa. Against that edifice, what is urged for is that configuration which does things anew, even instantiating X in another mode, and it comes through what Jeremy Glick (2016, 19) marks as the axis of 'combination' and 'recombination'.

The uprooting of the black from being, making the black lost (without identity, belonging and being), is what is combated. The roots of blackness, without the obsession with the idea of purity, the problem of pure being as Nahum Chandler (2014) notes, but with the effort of reconfiguration, is the force that lies in rupture. The presentation of X, which turns out to be a reconfiguration, is telling when Slavoj Žižek (2014, 133) points to the acts that 'seize the opening provided by the X – an unknown new (lack of) identity engendered by the very process of enslavement that has ensured those roots were forever lost'. But being preoccupied with the concepts of the 'void' and 'Void proper', the conclusion that Žižek (2014, 413) reaches is that X is in plenitude at the starting point. The two voids are at the level of ontology. Žižek (2014, 413) writes: 'The zero-level, the starting point, is not zero but less than zero, a pure minus without positive terms with regard to which it would function as a lack/excess'. At the level of the void there is that antagonism of nothing, of nothingness – pure inactivity/non-event. What happens in politics, then, where X causes rupture in the interstices? This is not a matter of ontological entities appearing and disappearing. X marks what is not in the void, and the place where X is in the world. Žižek is correct to point to the field of antagonism at the level of inscription and erasure, where the condition is the invention of the void. But this void is not a given where there is, according to Žižek (2014, 414), 'a virtual/spectral substanceless X that supplements actual objects, filling the void in the heart of reality'. What Žižek insists upon is that different take which suggests that X is a *tabula rasa*.

X here is in a relationship of antagonism with the subject (read white qua whiteness, and also antiblack). Accordingly, the subject's preoccupation is, for Žižek (2014, 415), an 'anamorphic inscription into reality'. The void, then, is determined by the subject and by X, which is reduced and obliterated in that void or, if it is deemed to exist, is a mere supplement (thus deemed to have no sense of determinative power). The subject comes to know itself through the encounter with the object. This is at the level of relation, and in some form of asymmetry. But the encounter of the subject and X (which is the void, or excess, even) is wholly different. The self-knowing of the subject is, in relation to X, that of mastery, domination over X, its inferiorization. If X emerges, then just as in the field of antagonism, it 'comes to exist as a pure gap' (Žižek 2014, 404).

The black as X in an antiblack world is a category of meaning, but also an abstraction. That meaning is an imposition, and X is the classification and hierarchization of the black in the domain of nothingness. This is the logic that justifies the void as something that is constitutive of the black.

The X which is something, the X of blackness of being à la Marriott (2018a), the one that emerges from the interstice, is in antagonism with the subject as it is the act that has reconfigured itself through intramural discursive engagements. X derives from Žižek's articulation of the proper name. According to Grant Farred (2011), things must be called by their proper names. There is a need for specificity in order to avoid the blanket referents 'all', 'us', 'we' and so on. Derrida (1976, 112) argues that giving names creates the possibility of not only pronouncing them, but also forbidding their pronouncement. He argues that this lies in the power to suspend their 'vocative absolute'. Extending this idea, Fred Moten (2018a, 153) writes: 'These names move and work within a history of such naming, a history of radical imagining and imagination that troubles the aesthetic and the political like a scar, like a choke-cherry tree'.

In calling for the forbidden and suspended aspect, Farred (2011, 166) insists that 'the "proper name", if it is to take its rightful place in the thinking of an event, cannot be made pallid'. For X to call things by their 'proper name', to name the condition of its dehumanization by its proper name, means that the proper name is naming things for what they are, and the attitudinal stance taken in the articulation and expression of critique makes it clear from where one is speaking. In fact, the importance of the 'proper name' is to specify the mode of address and its pointed directionality. The name is not only the device of identification, but also an inventory, an opening. To name is the act of self-determination (owing to one's own freedom). X moves and dwells in everything that is in favour of liberation. It is important to state clearly to whom the address is directed and in what name. Here, as a matter of disposition, X is the 'proper name' against the interpellative liberalism that pervades post-1994 South Africa. The problematic that X is dealing with is, as Wilderson (2020) states, one in the proper name of meta-aporia. Thinking in the domain of the problem for thought, as Chandler (2014) elucidates, is not avoiding the problem but subjecting it to problematization. This is helpful for understanding X in relation to the modes of instantiation that Farred (2011, 166) calls the 'jarring moment'. It is the event that happens in the moment of unfolding, the interstice. The opening, here, in its radical form, is conceptualized by Farred (2011, 169) as the 'declarative undercut' where X can be reconfigured to be that axe, its cut that undoes and mows down the absolute and the erect. This declarative undercut is revelatory, and it is a clear mark of the interstice. It is a cut against the cult – that is, the result of the latter being the 'unconscious consensus' of liberal conformism where all must think in ways that toe the line (Wilderson 2020, 12). The declarative undercut is the principality of blackness. It also means the opening, what Glick (2016, 24) terms the 'relay-circuit', a place where rupture is incubated and actualized. This principality is also in the interrogative gesture – that is, the very idea of the cut to mark rupture. It is then unfolded in two forms that Farred (2011, 161) distinguishes as 'wretched' and 'wretchedness'. Also insisting on the principality of the interrogative spirit, Farred argues that the two concepts are not the same. In the condition of X, the distinction goes, on the one hand, to the idea of South Africa, where X is an invention of conquest to mark the nothingness of blackness as the figure of representation, and, on the other hand, to the word and world of Azania as the reconfiguration of the blackness of being, where X is the name of the black in its own modes of discourse and radical imagination. So, taking Farred's distinction in line with this elucidation, wretchedness is the idea of South Africa and wretched is the word and world of Azania for those who insist on another reality. To that effect, wretchedness should not prevail. This is because it is antithetical to the word and world of Azania. What X still marks is what Farred (2011, 171) emphatically proposes thus: 'Always, "wretched" must do battle against "wretchedness"'. More (2015–2016, 103) further charges: 'In point of fact, liberation cannot be given. It has to be fought for'. This, indeed, is the mark of rupture, a domain of extended thought.

In the interstice, X erupts as the radical opening, that openness. Derrida has the interstice in mind when he states:

> This hollow space is not an opening among others. It is opening itself, the opening of opening, that which can be enclosed within no category or totality, that is, everything within experience which can no longer be described by traditional concepts, and which resists every philosopheme. (Derrida 1978, 73)

X is located in the interstice that marks a fundamental distinction between knowing and the making of language (Moten 2018b). Žižek (1989, 95) writes: 'Ideological space is made of non-bound, non-tied elements, "floating signifiers", whose very identity is "open", overdetermined by their articulation in a chain with other elements – that is, their "literal" signification depends on their metaphorical surplus signification'. But what then occurs is what Žižek calls the 'ideological quilt', which reverses the whole ideological field. 'The quilting performs the totalization by means of which this free floating of ideological elements is halted, fixed – that is to say, by means of which they become parts of the structured network of meaning' (Žižek 1989, 95–96). To quilt the whole ideological field, just like the decadence of colonial reasoning, is to ensure that it is reducible and fixed to the totalizing nature of the dominant force in play. In this sense, there is no openness but only foreclosure. This is what Žižek (1991, 68) sees as a 'closed whole', as the conditions of possibility are denied to impose impossibility. It is against this stasis that openness is insisted upon. 'Every partial moment, so to speak, "truncated from within" . . . cannot fully become "itself", it cannot ever reach "its own place", it is marked with an inherent impediment, and it is this impediment which "sets in motion" the dialectical development' (Žižek 1991, 68).

The mark of freedom
Moving beyond what Žižek gestures to, and in a space where the necessity of freedom is valued, Moten (2003, 26) opposes enclosure and insists on freedom. This is drawn from his effort to dwell in 'theoretical senses' that will make value from what has not been valued. This, for Moten, is the very idea of the 'freedom drive' that is liberatory and accelerative. And, in the case of containment and closure, it 'cuts' – that is, it makes a breakthrough for improvisation to reign. As Moten (2003, 41) eloquently puts it, 'such production – such radically ensemblic, radically improvisational objection – is the unfinished, continually re-engendered, actively re-engendering of the black (and blue and sentimental) avant-garde'. This avant-garde spirit engenders X, and as a form of radical performance, of insisting on living, of doing politics proper, it is expansive in its drive to render the interstices more open – blurred. According to Moten, the 'freedom drive' is the

very grounding of black performance in its avant-garde desire to be free, since the very idea of being free is inseparable from the avant-garde. Therefore, X is the mark of freedom. It is the freedom drive that stems from Robin Kelley's (2002) 'freedom dreams' that are still being dreamt in tragedy. These are the dreams that propel the interstices to rupture. This rupture, Moten (2018a, 160) appositely affirms, is 'how the underground operates out in, and as, the open'. Freedom dreams inform the ways of being and also being-in-freedom – that is, fighting for freedom even in its continued denial. Freedom dreams stem from what Kelley (2002, 150) calls 'the black radical imagination'. 'It is fundamentally a product of struggle, of victories and losses, crises and openings, and endless conversations circulating in a shared environment' (Kelley 2002, 150). Of its parallel in the name of the black radical tradition, Moten writes:

> The black radical tradition improvises terror . . . in ways that don't limit terror's discursive or cultural trace to an exclusive descriptive approach toward some either immediately present or heretofore concealed truth. There is also a prescriptive component in this tradition, which is to say in its narrative and in its narratives, that cuts the mythic and/or objectifying structures and effects of narrative while at the same time always holding onto resources that flow from narration's partnership with description. (Moten 2018a, 41–42)

The black radical tradition is the force of rupture, what Cedric Robinson (2000) defines as the critique of Western civilization. This is the critique of what is indefensible. The continuous rupture of X, then, in this extended thought, breaks through and transcends the closures that valorize this Western civilization. Even if the results are tragic, more so in the failure of this critique, there is no stopping. The will to begin is where the value of the opening is. It is the refusal to accept closure. It is the will for a different set of conditions, the radical possibility in the effort of the freedom drive and the fact of its inspiration being drawn from freedom dreams. It is the freedom drive and freedom dreams that, in the Fanonian spirit, Glick (2016, 215) articulates as 'an idea of radical generosity'. This attitude, which Nelson Maldonado-Torres (2008a, 8) refers to as a 'decolonial attitude', is the one that is grounded in the radical acts of love whose phenomenological grounding is giving the other and giving oneself, even in the midst of being dispossessed of that very gift. X, in this (un)fold(ing), is engaged in what to Glick (2016, 215) is a reconfiguration that is 'always a retroactive procedure'. Since X has been the origin of what is an arbitrary sign, a thing not worthy of having a name attached to it, the act of reconfiguration changes the whole signifying field, and it is the field that those who embody X cultivate themselves, so that they always revitalize the modes of their existential struggle.

Against bounded reasoning

The radical effort to challenge closure still ensues. The conceptual arrest and eclipse of form and content are refuted to create conditions that allow what Moten (2018b, 124) refers to as 'necessary and irreducible openness', which intensifies the black point of view as its own point of view. This is the scripting that stands against the closed statutes that call for the interpretation informed by what Mogobe Ramose (2007, 311) calls 'bounded reasoning', which clearly means being caught on the inside of the law while claiming to be critical of it – being on the pendulum of exclusion and inclusion while being excluded – being marked out(side). Bounded reasoning inaugurates and perpetuates conquest;

such reasoning can even claim to be its antithesis. Bounded reasoning never undoes what it purports to undo, but reifies it. What stands erect, as the result of this decadent reasoning, is what Ramose remarks on eloquently thus:

> Impermeable boundaries are totally and completely impermeable boundaries. Impermeable boundaries are totally sealed enclosures or circles. They do not allow for the possibility of change of identity resulting from existential influences. Their response to existential necessity to relate to the external world tends to proceed from the assumption that its identity is the only one, and most important relative to all other possibilities. In this sense, impermeable boundaries are inward-looking and absolutist. (Ramose 2007, 322)

This is the 'the figural darkness of this X' and here Marriott (2018b, 397) states that the 'black is forced to darken its own language of innocence'. According to Marriott, in political work being and thought do not have that full ontological status. These are in the making as they are being fought for. They are, in the case of X qua blackness, not a given, as they are structurally interdicted. It is in the interstice of interdiction that what Moten (2018b, 102) calls 'dark speech', whose function is to combat the 'executive speech', emerges, and it is in that speech that Marriott (2018b, 420) says that 'blackness is beyond any grasp of ontology, and indeed of representation'. It is that thing that is negativized and eliminated not only in the realm of the things that are sentient. It is the banality of the racist tropes that insists on the nothingness of the black, and that there is nothing worthy of feeling and sentiment there. All forms of violent fantasies and their actualization find justification when directed towards the black. The nothingness of the black means that ethical concerns, and even common sense, will not come to the rescue by making it clear that the black is human. The codes of ontological destruction still stand, are even intensified, to ensure that there is no language that will account for the black having been wronged, and that all there is to it is to stand with the logics of the dehumanization of the black as the reality, the way things are – and nothing can be done about that.

A challenge to the last instance

The inscriptive laws have been the violation of X. Since X, for Marriott, has the capacity to complicate what is true and false through the power of reconfiguration, of generating its own meaning, it stands in relation to the power of erasure that is still there in writing. The political destiny of the black, which is often pre/overdetermined in the colonial condition, has made it its practice to erase the black. The black, rendered nothing, 'can be substituted, overturned, suspended, and reversed by a mere stroke of a pen' (Marriott 2018b, 369). But in the scene of writing, this 'scenography', as Chandler (2014, 3) calls it, 'nothing comes on the scene punctually'. This is where X writes, in its avant-garde spirit, the blackness of being; this scene makes X be both a sign and politics, and not the first or the last instance. Marriott (2018b, 387), in challenging the 'trope of the last instance', argues for X as not being bound by closure, even though it is lurking everywhere in the writing and politics of X. By insisting on rupture and offering a challenge to the last instance, Marriott insists:

> At issue is the paradox of what is both necessary and insufficient when the last instance remains, and what

is *really* first can only later be grasped *after* its historic fall into representation, and where what is considered a cause is actually the effect of an effect, and what is considered an effect can present itself only as the cause of a cause that has no guarantee or alibi other than the error or deception. (Marriot 2018b, 387, emphasis in the original)

Indeed, X is not a foreclosure. It is a fated opening. Marriott continues:

Similarly, the question of *when* is the last instance, experienced here as something awaited and infinitely suspended, is probably not the same issue as to whether, in its utterance, the last instance is always represented by what it presupposes, by way of return, or whether such rhetoric invariably produces what in the first instance it is supposed to represent but only via the detour of representation. (Marriot 2018b, 388)

The radical opening of X, as the radical inscription, the mark that bears a resemblance to the interstice of form (which has been subjected to closure), is one that is reconfigured here to liberate form.

Thus, by definition, it is always first and last. It is first . . . because like the strange fruit it is, its flesh ripens through the expiration of its contents, and [its] skin envelops nothing more than an absence blossoming. But it is also last, because its fall is never able to reach representation, for like the hung, irresolved thing it is, it is held up by the rope of nonexistence and thereupon hangs suspended before the law of its being. (Marriott 2018b, 390)

The problem of the last instance is one of slippages, because there is nothing to it in so far as X is concerned. The last instance connotes the over/determining instance, and this is what X is militating against. The blackness of being is always, in the reconfiguration of X, a differential becoming. For, there are no guarantees. Everything is in what Glick (2016, 109) refers to as 'radical flux'. This is that movement of 'before' and 'after', 'beginning' and 'end', which does not resolve by being brought into reconfiguration that then becomes the generative force of what X is, not in its meaning but in its operation in the field of thought – that is, what can be called the 'metamorphosis of the body', which José Gil (1998, 197) locates in the ontological field and as the rupturous invention. This fitting characteristic applies as well to what Gil (1998, 11) criticizes as that which 'soaks up the impetus of the force that it comes from and tends to make it disappear'. X, as the very critical function of the operator, the operative force, the rupture of the interstice, has led Gil (1998, 12) to ask: 'Now, what "work" does the operator do?' Christina Sharpe (2016, 13) has a snappy answer: 'Wake work'.

For Glick (2016, 178), there is a 'revolutionary prior' and just as for Marriott (2018b), it is not the first instance which will teleologically lead to the last. Rather, the prior is the marker of the opening, whether there is success in *firsts* or failure, or success or failure in the last instance. The prior lies in what X is, in fact, when the interstice is ruptured. Glick (2016, 178) writes: 'Such revolutionary priors do not stifle action or freeze action in a static mold of nostalgia but rather enrich the clarity of execution'. There are, in X, leaps and falls in what Marriott (2018b, 386) calls 'the potential world of the X . . . black writing becomes the expression of what might be possible in the writing down of the world'. This is the very idea of reconfiguration. The locus of thought lies in 'the pivotal *first*', that locus of rupture, the intra-mural communal hold: 'the shift *from* innocence to difference thus literally becomes the politics of politics' (Marriott 2018b, 409, emphasis in the original). This is where the first and not the last instance is that rupture against enclosure.

J. Kameron Carter (2019) announces and marks what he calls 'black malpractice', where X knows, thinks and does from its own statement and testament of being outside the law's regulation of speech. Indeed, black malpractice is neither elab-oration of the law, nor its interpretation of statutes, but their blurring.

Black malpractice, as Carter aptly argues, can be said to be the reconfiguration of X. In fact, black malpractice is X. With this modest provocation, what is engaged, in forms of justifica-tion, solidifies the investigation at hand. Those who are unjustly (ill-/mis)treated are deemed unjust when they stand up for themselves in the name of justice. They are always interdicted in whatever they think, know and do. They are told how and what to think. They are told what they know is not true. They are told what they do is wrong. They are told not to try to change things and they must leave things the way they are. They are told not to 'disturb the peace'. They are told to be civil. They are told to be reasonable. They are told to be fair. They are told to stop complaining. They are told not to stay in the past. They are told to move on. They are told to take responsibility. They are told they are the problem. They are told . . .

Yes, those who are told. They are treated like children, and should they claim any form of self-determination, that gets inter-dicted. For, as Kathryn Yussoff (2019, 3) notes, 'they are coded into colonial possession through dispossession'. Being at the receiving end of dispossession of land, labour and humanity, of what has made them X, they are interdicted when they reconfigure themselves and take that X and act on it in liberatory ways. Only those who refuse to be told, who know what is at stake, will not listen to what they are told by those who conquered them. The author of freedom, the black, exists to own that freedom, and it is thus justifiable for the black to insist on it in the tragedy of its absence. This is still the reality. The black continues to live in unfreedom. The tragedy is even worse if the expectation is that the conqueror will bring this freedom. As X, the black is its own liberator.

In order to make liberation possible, the black will take a non-apologetic stance towards black malpractice. If whiteness is the sacred, having arrogated to itself all that is divine, it is from black malpractice that the black qua X will not bow to what whiteness expects things to be in the white supremacist world. X in black malpractice denotes those who do not give a damn, as they are damned. From this stance, the insurrectionary political inflection is not hard to detect, not far off. It is the insurrection against the very interdiction of what claims to be politics proper – the practice. The idea of property is rebelled against. Those who are depoliticized are reconfiguring themselves: what comes into being is X – the figure of politics qua politics. Carter (2019, 69) argues for X as that which 'indexes sacrality', that which confronts and exceeds the colonial enclosure. The mysticism of dissimulation, this diabolical coloniality, gets unmasked; this is what X produces endlessly to become what 'the violent homogeneity of ontopoliticality cannot hold' (Carter 2019, 71). X is, according to Carter (2019, 71), the 'unholdable', 'unhavable', 'incapturable' – what the polity of whiteness cannot subject to its liberal conformism.

X as 'black radical malpractice', 'black radical deviance', 'the black radical sacred', Carter's (2019, 74) addition to the reconfiguration of the tradition – the black radical tradition, the black radical imagination, the black radical tragic and so on – bears a different consent and political accent and accentuation. Black malpractice is reconfiguration absolute – X – it is exhaustive insistence on what Brent Edwards (2017, 27) refers to as 'scat', the literal dropping of words, the scat produced by the inside, what is inaudible to those who are outside this intramural commune. What is pejoratively declared 'nonsense' in scat is what, for Edwards, is of value. Scat and X, in the realm of the senses, or the 'common sense' of the 'unconscious consensus' (Wilderson 2020, 12), is what eludes capture. This finds warm embrace in Moten (2003, 67), who calls for the sacredness of that 'ensemble of the senses from which it springs and which it stimulates' – that is, in its praise. Scat, for Edwards (2017), is what is not captured in words. For, as Moten (2003) states, scat is the place where words cannot go. It is, according to Nathaniel Mackey (2018, 193), 'nonspeech' – that is to say, among other things, that the realm of conventional speech is not sufficient for saying what needs to be said. Scat is rupture, an opening of the unutterable – that is, if it is where words cannot go, should they insist, they will not reach that place. As Edwards (2017, 56) notes, scat 'liquefies words' – it defies articulation and transcription. Black malpractice qua scat is 'apophatic unsaying' – what Carter (2019, 83) frames as the poetics of the category of the unsaid which 'releases a freedom that is illegible within the terms of politicality'.

Towards reconfiguration

Plainly, this blackness, in all ways and forms of its figurations and reconfigurations, is the word and world of Azania. Whatever that blackness is will always stay as the very paradox that still haunts X. To say blackness qua X is the very principality of the *first*. The cartography of blackness magisterially scripted above clearly affirms the protocols of openness. There is no final destination. This serves as a reminder of the black radical imaginative inscriptions whose projects of freedom come from different principalities; and based on their lived experience, their thought, blackness remains open. It is this radical opening of X that originates from what Marriott (2018a) names as the blackness of being. It is this being as not absolute, but one in the making in order to end the world that dehumanizes the very being of X. Chandler (2014, 111, emphasis in the original) comes in handy here: 'This complex passage and way of inhabitation remains for us, here, now, only by way of this mark, this remainder, perhaps, *of* X'. Chandler illuminates matters further in locating X as a matter of thought, what matters in thought, and what matters most in the contemporary thought as a 'problem' for thought, as lived in principalities of black inscription: blackness writing itself in its own name – *in-itself* and *for-itself* – is the task of reconfiguration at hand – a complex one, indeed. It is complex in so far as it is not teleological. What it can lead to is uncertainty, and it is this risky affair that makes the existential struggle an ongoing one. What is desired and wanted is what should be worked for. By way of reconfiguration, there is that new dimension in place and it has no permanence, as the condition that it is in demands the constant creation of other modalities of being.

This matter of reconfiguration is the matter of this X-File.

That is why this X-File is the radical opening of that first instance, the thought that will forever go beyond it, as thinking is continuing in ways that do not settle for answers but launch intensive investigations in various registers to open many other vistas. This file is just one entry point to this opening. This file, the content of thought, its reconfiguration, sets out the ways in which X can be thought as the thinking, knowing and doing of blackness – the blackness of being. Thought here does not mean thinking X as the object of thought, but as its site, its generative place – the rupture of the interstice. It is from X that the blackness of being issues as the statement and testament that deliver critique and affirm ways of knowing, doing and thinking which radically insist on being free.

The composition of X, as the result of it being reconfigured, is the principality of extended thought. Since this is not the obsession with the assimilationist gesture of 'we are human too', but the composition of X as the reaffirmation that springs from the intramural commune, it seeks no recognition from the white gaze. Nor is X the appeal for the white gaze to change the way it sees things. This is not the matter of concern. X is *for-itself* and *in-itself*.

The word and world of Azania, as thought by X, is a radical possibility. The insistent demand is for the Azania that is free. X will remain forever haunting, a bane to what refuses it. With its language to come, with its being to come, with its land to come, with all that has to do with being genuinely liberated to come, this coming is the one which cannot be deferred to the future. The living present is the one that demands Azania must come into being. Azania is the now.

References

Agamben, Giorgio. 1998. *Homo Sacer: Sovereign Power and Bare Life*. Translated by Daniel Heller-Roazen. Stanford: Stanford University Press.

Alcoff, Linda M. 1991. 'The Problem of Speaking for Others'. *Cultural Critique* 20: 5–32.

Alexander, Amanda S. 2004. 'Not the Democracy We Struggled For: The Landless People's Movement and the Politicization of Urban-Rural Division in South Africa'. Honours thesis, Harvard College.

Armah, Ayi Kwei. 1984. 'Masks and Marx: The Marxist Ethos vis-à-vis African Revolutionary Theory and Praxis'. *Présence Africaine* 131: 35–65.

Barthes, Roland. 1982. *Empire of Signs*. Translated by Richard Howard. New York: Hill and Wang.

Barthes, Roland. 2015. *'The "Scandal" of Marxism' and Other Writings on Politics*. Translated by Chris Turner. London: Seagull Books.

Biko, Steve. 1978. *I Write What I Like*. Oxford: Heinemann.

Böhmke, Henrick. 2010a. 'The Branding of Social Movements in South Africa'. *Dispositions* 1 (April). https://heinrichbohmke.com/2013/05/branding/, accessed 21 May 2023.

Böhmke, Henrick. 2010b. 'The White Revolutionary as a Missionary? Contemporary Travels and Researches in Caffraria'. *New Frank Talk* 5: 9–28.

Callinicos, Alex. 1989. 'Marxism and the National Question'. *Education for Socialists* 7: 4–21.

Carter, J. Kameron. 2019. 'Black Malpractice (A Poetics of the Sacred)'. *Social Text* 37 (2): 67–107.

Césaire, Aimé. 1972. *Discourse on Colonialism*. Translated by Joan Pinkham. New York: Monthly Review Press.

Chandler, Nahum D. 2014. *X: The Problem of the Negro as a Problem for Thought*. New York: Fordham University Press.

Copeland, Huey. 2016. 'Tending-Towards-Blackness'. *October* 156 (Spring): 141–144.

Department of Finance. 1996. *Growth, Employment and Redistribution: A Macroeconomic Strategy*. Pretoria: Department of Finance, Republic of South Africa.

Derrida, Jacques. 1976. *Of Grammatology*. Translated by Gayatri C. Spivak. Baltimore: Johns Hopkins University Press.

Derrida, Jacques. 1978. *Writing and Difference*. London: Routledge and Kegan Paul.

Derrida, Jacques. 1993. *Aporias*. Translated by Thomas Dutoit. Stanford: Stanford University Press.

Derrida, Jacques. 2018. *Before the Law: The Complete Text of Préjugés*. Translated by Sandra van Reenen and Jacques de Ville. Minneapolis: University of Minnesota Press.

Edwards, Brent H. 2017. *Epistrophies: Jazz and the Literary Imagination*. Cambridge, MA: Harvard University Press.

Fanon, Frantz. 1965. *A Dying Colonialism*. Translated by Haakon Chevalier. New York: Grove Press.

Fanon, Frantz. 1967. *Black Skin, White Masks*. Translated by Charles L. Markmann. New York: Grove Press.

Fanon, Frantz. 1969. *The Wretched of the Earth*. Translated by Constance Farrington. Harmondsworth: Penguin Books.

Farley, Anthony P. 1997. 'The Black Body as Fetish Object'. *Oregon Law Review* 7: 457–535.

Farley, Anthony P. 2002. 'The Poetics of Colorlined Space'. In *Crossroads, Directions and a New Critical Race Theory*, edited by Francisco Valdes, Jerome McCristal Culp and Angela P. Harris, 97–158. Philadelphia: Temple University Press.

Farley, Anthony P. 2003. 'B. Reason's Lure: The Enchantment of Subordination: *The Dream of Interpretation*'. *University of Miami Law Review* 57 (3): 686–725.

Farley, Anthony P. 2008. 'The Colorline as Capitalist Accumulation'. *Buffalo Law Review* 56: 953–963.

Farred, Grant. 2011. 'Wretchedness'. In *Living Fanon: Global Perspectives*, edited by Nigel Gibson, 158–172. Basingstoke: Palgrave Macmillan.

Freire, Paulo. 1994. *Pedagogy of the Oppressed*. New York: Continuum.

Gil, José. 1998. *Metamorphosis of the Body*. Translated by Stephen Mueke. Minneapolis: University of Minnesota Press.

Glick, Jeremy M. 2016. *The Black Radical Tragic: Performance, Aesthetics, and the Unfinished Haitian Revolution*. New York: New York University Press.

Glissant, Édouard. 1997. *Poetics of Relation*. Translated by Betsy Wing. Ann Arbor: University of Michigan Press.

Gordon, Lewis R. 1995. *Bad Faith and Antiblack Racism*. New York: New Humanity Books.

Gordon, Lewis R. 2000. *Existentia Africana: Understanding Africana Existential Thought*. London: Routledge.

Gordon, Lewis R. 2008. 'A Phenomenology of Biko's Black Consciousness'. In *Biko Lives: Contesting the Legacies of Steve Biko*, edited by Andile Mngxitama, Amanda Alexander and Nigel C. Gibson, 83–93. Basingstoke: Palgrave Macmillan.

Grosfoguel, Ramon. 2016. 'What is Racism?' *Journal of World-Systems Research* 22 (1): 9–15.

Hadfield, Leslie A. 2016. *Liberation and Development: Black Consciousness Community Programs in South Africa*. East Lansing: Michigan University Press.

Hall, Ruth. 2003. 'A Comparative Analysis of Land Reform in South Africa and Zimbabwe'. In *Unfinished Business: The Land Crisis in Southern Africa*, edited by Margaret C. Lee and Karen Colvard, 255–285. Pretoria: Africa Institute of South Africa.

Hall, Ruth. 2004a. *Land and Agrarian Reform in South Africa: A Status Report, 2004*. Research report no. 20. Cape Town: PLAAS, University of the Western Cape.

Hall, Ruth. 2004b. 'A Political Economy of Land Reform in South Africa'. *Review of African Political Economy* 31 (100): 213–222.

Hall, Ruth. 2009. 'Land Reform's Middle Ground'. *Mail & Guardian*, 31 July–6 August: 13.

Han, Sora. 2015a. *Letters of the Law: Race and the Fantasy of Colorblindness in American Law*. Stanford: Stanford University Press.

Han, Sora. 2015b. 'Slavery as Contract: *Betty's Case* and the Question of Freedom'. *Law and Literature* 27 (3): 395–416.

Hartman, Saidiya. 1997. *Scenes of Subjection: Terror, Slavery and Self-Making in Nineteenth-Century America*. Oxford: Oxford University Press.

Hartman, Saidiya and Frank B. Wilderson III. 2003. 'The Position of the Unthought'. *Qui Parle* 13 (2): 182–201.

Heidegger, Martin. 1962. *Being and Time*. Translated by John Macquarrie and Edward Robinson. New York: Harper and Row.

Hesse, Barnor. 2011. 'Marked Unmarked: Black Politics and the Western Political'. *South Atlantic Quarterly* 110 (4): 974–984.

The Invisible Committee. 2017. *Now*. Translated by Robert Hurley. South Pasadena: Semiotext(e).

Jackson, George. 1972. *Blood in My Eye*. Baltimore: Black Classic Press.

Ka Plaatjie, Thami. 2003. 'Taking Matters into Their Own Hands: The Indigenous African Response to the Land Crisis in South Africa, 1990–2001'. In *Unfinished Business: The Land Crisis in Southern Africa*, edited by Margaret C. Lee and Karen Colvard, 287–316. Pretoria: Africa Institute of South Africa.

Kelley, Robin D.G. 2002. *Freedom Dreams: The Black Radical Imagination*. Boston: Beacon Press.

Kunene, Buhle. 2019. '"Land or Death": BLF Fails to Defend Slogan'. *Mail & Guardian*, 12 June. https://mg.co.za/article/2019-06-12-00-land-or-death-blf-fails-to-defend-slogan/.

Lenin, Vladimir I. 1962. *On Socialist Ideology and Culture*. Moscow: Progress Publishers.

Lenin, Vladimir I. 1980. *Marxism and Revisionism*. Moscow: Progress Publishers.

Lenin, Vladimir I. 1992. *The State and Revolution*. Harmondsworth: Penguin Books.

Lezra, Jacques. 2018. *On the Nature of Marx's Things: Translation as Necrophilology*. New York: Fordham University Press.

Mackey, Nathaniel. 2018. *Paracritical Hinge: Essays, Talks, Notes, Interviews*. Iowa City: University of Iowa Press.

Maldonado-Torres, Nelson. 2008a. *Against War: Views from the Underside of Modernity*. Durham, NC: Duke University Press.

Maldonado-Torres, Nelson. 2008b. 'Lewis Gordon: Philosopher of the Human'. *CLR James Journal* 14 (1): 103–137.

Mamdani, Mahmood. 1996. *Citizen and Subject: Contemporary Africa and the Legacy of Late Colonialism*. Princeton: Princeton University Press.

Mamdani, Mahmood. 2013. *Define and Rule: Native as Political Identity*. Johannesburg: Wits University Press.

Manganyi, N. Chabani. 1973. *Being-Black-in-the-World*. Johannesburg: Sprocas/Ravan Press.

Manganyi, N. Chabani. 1977. *Mashangu's Reverie and Other Essays*. Johannesburg: Ravan Press.

Marriott, David. 2000. *On Black Men*. New York: Columbia University Press.

Marriott, David. 2007. *Haunted Life: Visual Culture and Black Modernity*. New Brunswick: Rutgers University Press.

Marriott, David. 2018a. *Whither Fanon: Studies in the Blackness of Black*. Stanford: Stanford University Press.

Marriott, David. 2018b. 'The X of Representation: Rereading Stuart Hall'. *Qui Parle* 27 (2): 356–430.

Marx, Karl. 1968a. 'Thesis on Feuerbach'. In *Karl Marx and Frederick Engels: Selected Works in One Volume*, 28–30. New York: International Publishers.

Marx, Karl. 1968b. 'The Eighteenth Brumaire of Louis Bonaparte'. In *Karl Marx and Frederick Engels: Selected Works in One Volume*, 97–180. New York: International Publishers.

Marx, Karl. 1976. *Capital*. Volume One. Translated by Ben Fowkes. Harmondsworth: Penguin Books.

Marx, Karl and Frederick [Friedrich] Engels. 1968. 'Manifesto of the Communist Party'. In *Karl Marx and Frederick Engels: Selected Works in One Volume*, 35–63. New York: International Publishers.

Memmi, Albert. 1965. *The Colonizer and the Colonized*. Boston: Beacon Press.

Mignolo, Walter D. 2011. *The Darker Side of Western Modernity: Global Futures, Decolonial Options*. Durham, NC: Duke University Press.

Mills, Charles W. 1997. *The Racial Contract*. Ithaca: Cornell University Press.

Mngxitama, Andile. 2001. 'Farm Workers: Citizens Without Rights: The Unfinished National Question'. Paper presented at the Southern Africa Regional Poverty Network Conference on Land

Reform and Poverty Alleviation in Southern Africa, Human Sciences Research Council, Pretoria, 4–5 June.

Mngxitama, Andile. 2004. 'South Africa's Land Reform: A Device to Forget?' Unpublished paper.

Mngxitama, Andile. 2006. 'The Taming of Land Resistance: Lessons from the National Land Committee'. *Journal of Asian and African Studies* 41 (1–2): 39–69.

Mngxitama, Andile. 2009. 'Blacks Can't be Racist'. *New Frank Talk* 3: 1–32.

Moodley, Kogila. 1991. 'The Continued Impact of Black Consciousness'. In *Bounds of Possibility: The Legacy of Steve Biko and Black Consciousness*, edited by N. Barney Pityana, Mamphele Ramphele, Malusi Mpumlwana and Lindy Wilson, 143–152. Cape Town: David Philip.

More, Mabogo P. 1996. 'Complicity, Neutrality or Advocacy: Philosophy in South Africa'. *Theoria* 87 (June): 124–135.

More, Mabogo P. 2004. 'Biko: Africana Existentialist Philosopher'. *Alternation* 11 (1): 79–108.

More, Mabogo P. 2005. 'Sartre and the Problem of Racism'. PhD thesis, University of South Africa.

More, Mabogo P. 2008. 'Biko: Africana Existentialist Philosopher'. In *Biko Lives: Contesting the Legacies of Steve Biko*, edited by Andile Mngxitama, Amanda Alexander and Nigel C. Gibson, 45–68. Basingstoke: Palgrave Macmillan.

More, Mabogo P. 2011. 'Fanon and the Land Question in (Post)apartheid South Africa'. In *Living Fanon: Global Perspectives*, edited by Nigel C. Gibson, 173–185. Basingstoke: Palgrave Macmillan.

More, Mabogo P. 2012. 'Black Consciousness Movement's Ontology: The Politics of Being'. *Philosophia Africana* 14 (1): 23–39.

More, Mabogo P. 2014. 'Locating Frantz Fanon in Post-Apartheid South Africa'. *Journal of Asian and African Studies* 49 (6): 1–15.

More, Mabogo P. 2015–2016. 'Biko and Douglass: Existential Conception of Death and Freedom'. *Philosophia Africana* 17 (2): 101–118.

More, Mabogo P. 2017. *Biko: Philosophy, Identity and Liberation*. Cape Town: HSRC Press.

Moten, Fred. 2003. *In the Break: The Aesthetics of the Black Radical Tradition*. Minneapolis: University of Minnesota Press.

Moten, Fred. 2018a. *Stolen Life*. Durham, NC: Duke University Press.

Moten, Fred. 2018b. *The Universal Machine*. Durham, NC: Duke University Press.

Moyo, Sam. 2007. 'The Land Question in Southern Africa: A Comparative View'. In *The Land Question in South Africa*, edited by Lungisile Ntsebeza and Ruth Hall, 60–84. Cape Town: HSRC Press.

Nancy, Jean-Luc. 2002. 'L'Intrus'. Translated by Susan Hanson. *CR: The New Centennial Review* 2 (3): 1–14.

Ntsebeza, Lungisile. 2005. 'Slow Delivery in South Africa's Land Reform Programme: The Property Clause Revisited'. Paper presented at the Harold Wolpe Memorial Lecture, University of KwaZulu-Natal, Pietermaritzburg, 24 August.

Ntsebeza, Lungisile. 2007. 'The Land Question in Southern Africa: A Comparative Review'. In *The Land Question in South Africa*, edited by Lungisile Ntsebeza and Ruth Hall, 60–84. Cape Town: HSRC Press.

Parliament of South Africa. 1913. *Natives Land Act (No. 27 of 1913)*. Cape Town: Parliament of South Africa.

Parliament of South Africa. 1936. *Native Trust and Land Act (No. 18 of 1936)*. Cape Town: Parliament of South Africa.

Parliament of South Africa. 1937. *Native Laws Amendment Act (No. 46 of 1937)*. Cape Town: Parliament of South Africa.

Parliament of South Africa. 1950. *Group Areas Act (No. 41 of 1950)*. Cape Town: Parliament of South Africa.

Parliament of South Africa. 1950. *Suppression of Communism Act (No. 44 of 1950)*. Cape Town: Parliament of South Africa.

Parliament of South Africa. 1951. *Bantu Authorities Act (No. 68 of 1951)*. Cape Town: Parliament of South Africa.

Parliament of South Africa. 1959. *Promotion of Bantu Self-Government Act (No. 46 of 1959)*. Cape Town: Parliament of South Africa.

Rabaka, Reiland. 2010. *Forms of Fanonism: Frantz Fanon's Critical Theory and the Dialectics of Decolonization*. Lanham: Lexington Books.

Ramose, Mogobe B. 1991. 'Self-Determination in Decolonisation'. In *Issues of Self-Determination*, edited by William Twining, 25–32. Aberdeen: Aberdeen University Press.

Ramose, Mogobe B. 2007. 'In Memoriam: Sovereignty and the "New" South Africa'. *Griffith Law Review* 16 (2): 310–329.

Ramose, Mogobe B. 2018. 'Towards a Post-Conquest South Africa: Beyond the Constitution of 1996'. *South African Journal of Human Rights* 34 (3): 326–341.

Republic of South Africa. 1967. *Terrorism Act (No. 83 of 1967)*. Cape Town: Republic of South Africa.

Republic of South Africa. 1973. *Gatherings and Demonstrations Act (No. 52 of 1973)*. Cape Town: Republic of South Africa.

Republic of South Africa. 1994. *White Paper on Reconstruction and Development (Notice No. 1954 of 1994)*. Cape Town: Republic of South Africa.

Republic of South Africa. 1996. *Constitution of the Republic of South Africa (Act No. 108 of 1996)*. Cape Town: Republic of South Africa.

Robinson, Cedric J. 2000. *Black Marxism: The Making of the Black Radical Tradition*. Chapel Hill: University of North Carolina Press.

Robinson, Cedric J. 2001. *An Anthropology of Marxism*. New York: Pluto Press.

Rosen-Carole, Adam. 2015. 'Demanding Politics'. *Kritike* 9 (1): 1–13.

Sartre, Jean-Paul. 1957. *Being and Nothingness: An Essay on Phenomenological Ontology*. Translated by Hazel E. Barnes. London: Methuen.

Sartre, Jean-Paul. 1964. *The Words*. Translated by Irene Clephane. London: Hamish Hamilton.

Sartre, Jean-Paul. 1965. *Anti-Semite and Jew*. Translated by George J. Becker. New York: Schocken Books.

Sexton, Jared. 2006. 'Race, Nation, and Empire in a Blackened World'. *Radical History Review* 95 (Spring): 250–261.

Sexton, Jared. 2015. 'Unbearable Blackness'. *Cultural Critique* 90 (Spring): 159–178.

Sharpe, Christina. 2016. *In the Wake: On Blackness and Being*. Durham, NC: Duke University Press.

South African Human Rights Commission. 2003. *4th Economic and Social Report, 2000/2002*. Johannesburg: South African Human Rights Commission.

Spillers, Hortense. 2003. *Black, White, and in Color: Essays on American Literature and Culture*. Chicago: University of Chicago Press.

Suárez-Krabbe, Julia. 2016. *Race, Rights and Rebels: Alternatives to Human Rights and Development from the Global South*. Lanham: Rowman and Littlefield International.

Thwala, Wellington D. 2002. 'Land and Agrarian Reform in South Africa'. Unpublished paper.

Trask, Haunani K. 2004. 'The Color of Violence'. *Social Justice* 31 (4): 8–16.

Turner, Lou. 2008. 'Self-Consciousness as Force and Reason of Revolution in the Thought of Steve Biko'. In *Biko Lives: Contesting the Legacies of Steve Biko*, edited by Andile Mngxitama, Amanda Alexander and Nigel C. Gibson, 68–82. Basingstoke: Palgrave Macmillan.

Vilakazi, Herbert W. 1980. 'Was Karl Marx a Black Man?' *Monthly Review* 2 (23): 42–60.

Warren, Calvin L. 2018. *Ontological Terror: Blackness, Nihilism, and Emancipation*. Durham, NC: Duke University Press.

Wauchope, George. 1984. 'Azania = Land of the Black People'. *Frank Talk*: 7–8. Unnumbered pamphlet.

Wilderson III, Frank B. 2003a. 'Black Marx: Whither the Slave in Civil Society'. *Social Identities* 9 (2): 225–240.

Wilderson III, Frank B. 2003b. 'The Prison Slave as Hegemony's (Silent) Scandal'. *Social Justice* 30 (2): 18–27.

Wilderson III, Frank B. 2008a. *Incognegro: Memoir of Exile and Apartheid*. Cambridge, MA: South End Press.

Wilderson III, Frank B. 2008b. 'Biko and the Problematic of Presence'. In *Biko Lives: Contesting the Legacies of Steve Biko*, edited by Andile Mngxitama, Amanda Alexander and Nigel C. Gibson, 96–114. Basingstoke: Palgrave Macmillan.

Wilderson III, Frank B. 2010. *Red, White, and Black: Cinema and the Structure of US Antagonisms*. Durham, NC: Duke University Press.

Wilderson III, Frank B. 2020. *Afropessimism*. New York: Liveright.

Wilson, Lindy. 1991. 'Bantu Stephen Biko: A Life'. In *Bounds of Possibility: The Legacy of Steve Biko and Black Consciousness*, edited by N. Barney Pityana, Mamphele Ramphele, Malusi Mpumlwana and Lindy Wilson, 15–77. Cape Town: David Philip.

Wynter, Sylvia. 1994. 'No Humans Involved: An Open Letter to My Colleagues'. *Forum N.H.I.* 1: 42–73.

Yusoff, Kathryn. 2019. 'White Utopia/White Inferno: Life on a Geologic Spike'. *E-Flux Journal* 97 (February): 1–13.

Ziarek, Ewa P. 2001. 'Rethinking Dispossession: On Being in One's Skin'. *Parallax* 7 (2): 3–19.

Žižek, Slavoj. 1989. *The Sublime Object of Ideology.* London: Verso.

Žižek, Slavoj. 1991. *For They Know Not What They Do: Enjoyment as a Political Factor.* London: Verso.

Žižek, Slavoj. 2014. *Absolute Recoil: Towards a New Foundation of Dialectic Materialism.* London: Verso.

Index

INDEX